广东省立中山图书馆 编著

老广州

In Search of Guangzhou Lost in Time

嶺南美術出版社

图书在版编目（CIP）数据

老广州 / 广东省立中山图书馆编著. —广州：岭南美术出版社，2009.8 （2022.10重印）
ISBN 978-7-5362-4116-9

Ⅰ.老… Ⅱ.广… Ⅲ.地方史—广州市—图集
Ⅳ.K296.51-64

中国版本图书馆CIP数据核字(2009)第081336号

策　　划：李昭醇
编　　著：倪俊明　蒋志华　周翠玲
英文翻译：映　青
封面题字：刘斯奋
策划编辑：翁少敏
责任编辑：翁少敏
责任技编：陆建豪　谢　芸
装帧设计：三瀚文化

老广州

出版、总发行：岭南美术出版社（网址：www.lnysw.net）
（广州市天河区海安路19号14楼 邮编：510627）
经　　销：全国新华书店
印　　刷：东莞市信誉印刷有限公司
版　　次：2009年8月第1版
印　　次：2022年10月第5次印刷
开　　本：787mm×1092mm　1/20
印　　张：17.5
印　　数：8501-10500册
ISBN 978-7-5362-4116-9

定　　价：58.00元

目录

CONTENTS

广州赋

刘斯奋

古之楚庭，今号穗城，二千年之华夏名都，广州居岭表而峥嵘。地滨南海，秦皇一统宇内而开郡；中原逐鹿，赵佗割据百越以称雄。其后九州复合，梅岭路通。移民土著，交往频密；南北文化，汇聚相融。遂使勃勃生机，涌动于炎方热土；蓬蓬活力，创业于往古来今。

广州之形胜也，云山重叠障其北，珠水浩荡襟其南，水阔则盛产鱼鳖虾蟹，山深则广栖走兽飞禽。于是百姓来集，以渔以猎；炎风播雨，宜牧宜耕。所喜民情务实而进取，俗尚节俭而劬勤，衣食渐给，生齿日增。遂有跨羊五仙，持穗来降，祝愿此区，永无饥荒。广州之民也，乃奋鹰扬之远志，发独出之遐想，因其地利，业兼农商。更揽大海于怀抱，趁风举而帆扬，输瓷器丝绸于外域，采特产奇货于异邦，开跨海贸易之先河，握致富金钥而自强。于是南洋商贾，亦闻风随至。一时黄木湾头，帆樯云集；波罗庙内，香火熙攘。奇装异服穿梭闹市，啁哳话语声动蕃坊[①]。又有花市龙船，疍歌飘色，摇神夺目，溢彩流光。宝玉易求，岑参诗篇称艳[②]；荔枝美味，东坡嗜之如狂[③]。主人宾客，饮馔游赏，其乐未央。若夫教化文明，亦蒸蒸日上。显宦大儒，光照青史；诗文书画，岭外名彰。更有达摩西来传法，于此登岸；六祖禅机深悟，开宗发扬。此自唐至清之事也，其间虽有南汉荒政，明末兵火，一旦疮痍洗净，仍是富庶之乡。

及至虎门销烟，史开近代。文明较量，骇浪惊涛。西来列强，船坚炮利；老大帝国，风雨飘摇。当此之时也，广州士民，危机先觉，奋起救亡，上下求索。前则鸦片战争，戊戌变法；后则辛亥革命，国共合作。更有广州起义一声惊雷，尽显英雄气魄。至于不甘落后，追赶潮流，西方文明，率先吸收；远赴海外，孜孜营求，实业兴国，未雨绸缪。此又广州人之所以为广州人也。

于是乎，历百年沧桑，东亚之睡龙复醒；尽驱豺虎，人民之共和国成。神州再造，曾经几番曲折；改革开放，一朝石破天惊。广州之民，遇亘古未有之良机，负披荆斩棘之使命，倚得天独厚之地利，持务实求真之秉性，义无返顾，奋身先行。三十年间，经济腾飞，社会巨变，奇迹屡创，鹏举青冥。

广州今之为城也，有十区之设，二市之辖④。南抵海角，北接韶关，东邻惠州、东莞，西则清远、佛山。若夫凌高天而四顾，但见人居稠密，绵延何止百里；机场如砥，起落无数航班；厂房棋布，多是高新科技；巨舶排岸，货箱屯积如山。更有明湖开镜，绿树连云。丽日临空，灿比珠玉；华灯彻夜，光夺星辰。气象之繁华，观瞻之雄壮，信其为岭南首府无让矣！

广州今之居人也，常住者七百万，流动者五百万。籍贯则四海五湖环球万国，行业则文体科卫工商士农。或身挟长技，或坐拥财雄，或穷则思变，或梦想登峰。风从云聚，行色匆匆。藉广州之舞台，施展拳脚；视羊城为福地，跃虎腾龙。得固欣然，挫亦不馁，期以不懈奋斗，搏取万一成功。

广州今之市面也，连云新筑，望衡接宇；八达通衢，入地盘空。滚滚车流如回翔雁阵，夜以继日；熠熠商场似琼楼玉宇，生意兴隆。琴棋书画，活跃社区文化；舞衫歌扇，繁荣艺术之宫。酒楼食肆遍于街巷，通宵达旦，无愧食在广州之美誉；姹紫嫣红百卉竞秀，四季不殊，尽显花城南国之情浓。若夫佳日闲暇，泛舟珠江，放眼处处木棉挺立，老榕低亚。兀兀长堤石凳，闪闪碧水晴空，昵昵红男绿女，嬉嬉白叟黄童。广州开埠至此，信知先人之血汗不负，人间之乐土可期矣！

祝曰：政府施政以人为本，社情民意在在关心，环保治安双管齐下，社会和谐共享太平。

2007年4月5日清明节

按：此文系《光明日报》《百城赋》系列之一，当时通过广州市委宣传部向广东省文联主席刘斯奋约稿。2007年4月23日发表。《广州日报》、《信息时报》等于次日转载。

注：

①白居易《琵琶行》诗："呕哑嘲哳难为听。"又：唐宋时于广州设"市舶司"，为我国历史上早之外贸管理机构。又在今光塔路一带设"蕃坊"，以居外国商客。

②岑参《送杨瑗尉南海》诗："海暗三山雨，花明五岭春。此乡多宝玉，慎莫厌清贫。"

③苏轼《食荔枝》诗："日啖荔枝三百颗，不辞长作岭南人。"

④广州市十区为：越秀、荔湾、番禺、天河、白云、海珠、黄埔、萝岗、南沙、花都，所辖二市为：从化、增城。

【开头语】

广州在日新月异地变化着，无论街市景观，还是民生世相，都与一个世纪甚至半个世纪前大不相同。古人说：逝者不可追。过去的时光固然一去不返，但逝去的一切总还藉着当日的文字与影像留下了一些不灭的印迹，悄然隐在那一排排一架架业已泛黄的陈旧书刊中。

十年前，我们在为读者提供咨询服务同时，陆续整理出一批旧广州图片资料，后将其中一部分选出，分作一百三十余个小题目，略作考述，集成《羊城寻旧》一书，于2004年春出版。

本书面世后，竟颇受读者欢迎，以至出版社多次加印，颇出乎我们意料。现应本书责任编辑翁少敏的要求，我们将原书文字做了部分修订，调整补充一些图片，并新增了英文译释。愿新面貌的《老广州》能助益更多的朋友了解认识广州的过去。

本书以一个个场景片段，串出老广州的大致面貌。读者在走马观花中看到的未必都是些浮光掠影，追寻过去也并非仅仅为了怀旧。在时光的长廊里，我们会有一种别样的视野，会得到一种参照。

1 【街市景观】

街道是城市的经络。穿越那些纵横交错的横衢通巷，我们可以捕捉到这个城市最富动感的姿态。从传统到现代，城市面貌变得异彩纷呈。在时光的流变中，广州街市的沧桑已成了我们记忆深处的一份收藏。

◎广州鸟瞰 An Aerial View of Guangzhou

“五岭北来峰在地，九州南尽水浮天”，以逶迤五岭为屏障的南粤大地，早在四五千年前的新石器时代，就开始了耕耘渔猎的文明进程。秦始皇三十三年（公元前214年），秦平岭南，南海郡尉任嚣筑任嚣城（亦称番禺城），开始了广州建城的历史。秦末汉初，赵佗据南岭天险，偏霸称帝，建立南越国，定都番禺。由此，奠定了广州作为岭南中心城市的地位，也肇始了与中原文明的契合过程。三国吴黄武五年（226年）析交州东部置广州，历史上始有了“广州”一名。南汉、南明两个封建王朝也先后在广州建都。

清末的广州。

Guangzhou in the late Qing Dynasty.

南天王陈济棠主粤，使20世纪30年代的广州出现了短暂的繁盛。

Guangzhou enjoyed a short prosperous period in 1930’s, owing to the governing of the Southern King Chen Jitang.

20 世纪 40 年代初的广州。

Guangzhou in early 1940's.

自秦汉以来，广州长期是郡治、州治、路治、府治、省治所在地，为广东政治、经济、文化中枢。1921 年，广州市政厅成立，正式设市，广州由此成为近代中国第一个城市型政区。新中国成立后，广州城市发展迅速，至 2000 年，市区面积已达 1443.6 平方公里。

20 世纪 60 年代初广州鸟瞰。

A bird's-eye view of Guangzhou in early 1960's.

◎城垣　City Wall of Guangzhou

广州城建历史肇始于秦始皇三十三年（公元前214年）的任嚣城。其后，广州城建设历经沧桑，不断拓展。南越扩建有赵佗城，东汉交州刺史步骘重建步骘城，南汉割据扩展新南城。至宋三百年间，循环地修子城、东城、西城，并在城南修雁翅城至江边。明代将宋元的子城、东城、西城三城合一，并在宋雁翅城上扩建新城。清初又在明新城东、南两侧增筑两翼。至此形成北倚越秀山镇海楼，南临五仙门、靖海门，东抵大东门，西达西门口的城垣格局。历经两千多年，广州中心城址一直不变，成就了众多的寻古访幽处。

拆城垣、辟马路，是广州近代市政建设的第一步。今天广州的许多道路在当时已经奠定了基础。图为在原城基上修建的一德路。

Turning city walls into streets is the first step in Guangzhou's modern construction. A lot of roads in Guangzhou were built this way long ago, such as Yide Road. shown here.

清代越秀山城垣，古城廓的旧事隐现如烟。

The city walls of Mt. Yuexiu in the Qing Dynasty seem to vaguely tell the history of this old city.

清末广州大北门，它曾经是北面进入广州的城门。

The Great North Gate of Guangzhou in the late Qing Dynasty used to be the northern entrance to the city.

随着军事防卫功能的式微，古老的城垣成了近代经济发展的障碍。1912年，广东军政府率先拆卸广州城正东门及大北门附近城墙。图为大北门附近城墙被拆时，瓦砾遍地的情景。

The old city walls have become obstacles to the modern city economic development because of their weakening function of military denfence. The Guangdong Military Government for the first time demolished the city walls in the East Gate and the Great North Gate in 1912, as we see here, the bricks and stones were all over the ground when the Great North Gate was removed.

1918年广州市政公所成立后，实施拆城墙筑马路，开始广州大规模的近代市政建设。图为被拆的部分城墙。

After setting up the Municial Department in 1918, Guangzhou began a large scale modern construction. This picture shows parts of the removed city walls.

◎珠江两岸 Pearl River Banks

“烟波如画舫如仙，珠江风月本无边。”作为广州母亲河的珠江，造就了从宋代的“珠江秋月”、“扶胥浴日”，直至当代的“珠水晴波”、“黄埔云樯”、“珠水夜韵”的无边景色，成为一处永不褪色的羊城胜景。

20 世纪 20 年代珠江江景。珠江西起鸦岗，东至莲花山，长 70 多公里，在广州市区穿流而过。

The Pearl River scenery in 1920's. The Pearl River, which flows through Guangzhou City, is over 70 kilometres long.It starts from Yagang in the west and ends at Mt.Lianhua in the east.

20 世纪 30 年代珠江岸上的建筑已颇具现代气息。大钟楼以英国天文台的乐曲报时，大新公司的天台游乐场有很多舶来的玩意。夕阳时分凭窗而立，可眺望浩渺的江面上渔火点点。

Even in 1930's, the buildings on the Pearl River seemed rather modern. The Great Clock Tower told the correct time by playing the same music as the British Observatory. The amusement centre on the top floor of the Daxin Company had a lot of foreign games. Boats were seen here and there on the wide river at sunset.

20 世纪 50 年代珠江上的帆影。

Boats on the Pearl River in 1950's.

◎海珠桥　The Haizhu Bridge

横跨珠江，自北岸的维新路（今广州起义路）口直达河南厂前街（今江南大道）的海珠桥，直到今天还是市内南北交通枢纽之一。它的建设动议始于清光绪年间，1929 年市设计委员会拟定了建筑计划，公开投标，终于以 103.2 万两白银的造价由美国慎昌洋行经办，由美国马克敦公司承建。1933 年 2 月 15 日建成通车。桥长 183 米，宽 18.3 米。建成后，开通了两条线路的公共汽车。

这是第一座连接市区珠江两岸的钢结构跨江大桥，它见证了数十年广州沧桑。而它本身也饱经风霜，1938 年日军侵占广州时，中段桥面开合部分被破坏；早先桥体中间是活动式以便于大船通过的景观只能在这张 1933 年的图片中看到了。

The Haizhu Bridge, which witnesses the history of Guangzhou, is the first steel bridge over the Pearl River in downtown Guangzhou. We can't see elsewhere except this precious picture taken in 1933 the opening and closing part in the middle of this bridge because it was destroyed when the Japanese army invaded Guangzhou in 1938.

1933 年 2 月 15 日，海珠桥通车典礼上，万头攒动、游人如织的场面。

Thousands of people on the inauguration and passing ceremony of the Haizhu Bridge on Feb. 15, 1933.

海珠桥桥面。桥身上“海珠桥”三个大字，为国民党元老胡汉民所书。

The three Chinese characters “Haizhu Bridge” on the bridge were original handwriting of Hu Hanming, the senior KMT Party member.

1949 年 10 月 14 日下午 5 时，国民党军队败退时炸毁了海珠桥。

The Haizhu Bridge was blown up at 5 PM, Oct, 14, 1949, by the KMT troops when they retreated in defeat.

广州市人民政府于 1950 年重建海珠桥。钢筋混凝土结构的桥身，尽管外观与原桥大致相仿，但桥面已不能开合。图为 1950 年海珠桥重建后举行通车典礼。领袖画像、红旗、标语，充满了那个时代的气息。

The Guangzhou People's Government rebuilt the Haizhu Bridge in 1950. Though the new steel concrete bridge looked almost the same as the original one, it could no longer open and close.The picture here shows the passing ceremony of the bridge in 1950 after being rebuilt. The pictures of leaders, red flags and slogans tell the rich flavour of that period of time.

1974 年底开始了海珠桥的扩建工程，1975 年 10 月正式竣工通车。扩建后的海珠桥，实现了三线行车，人车分流，新旧桥的建筑风格浑然一体。

The Haizhu Bridge was enlarged at the end of 1974. The project was completed and the bridge was open to vehicular traffic in October, 1975. After being rebuilt, the Haizhu Bridge had 3 lanes seperating vehicles form pedestrians. As we see here, the construction styles of the new and old bridges from a harmonious whole.

◎海珠广场　The Haizhu Square

海珠广场是广州最早的城市广场。1954年建成后一直是广州的一个标志性形象。它位于海珠桥北端，因地处旧时的海珠石附近，又紧靠海珠桥而得名。原址清代称菜栏和果栏，是城外的果菜集市。20 世纪 30 年代前后渐成民居。1938 年被日军飞机夷成平地。1949 年 10 月，国民党军队轰炸海珠桥，此地更成一片废墟。1951 年广州市人民政府在此地开始修建广场，1954 年建成。1959 年 10

1957 年的海珠广场，绿草如茵。

The Haizhu Square in 1957 was covered with green grass.

1963 年的海珠广场。

The Haizhu Square in 1963.

月，为纪念广州解放10周年，在广场北侧兴建由尹积昌创作的广州解放纪念像。20世纪60年代初，该雕塑以“珠海丹心”名列羊城八景之一。1969年雕像被拆除。1979年选用潘鹤、梁明诚设计的方案重建，次年7月落成。

1965年的海珠广场。
The Haizhu Square in 1965.

◎东山　Dongshan District

位于旧广州城东门外的东山，直至清末还是环境清幽的城郊，因明、清时期建有东山寺而得名。清末因广九铁路通过此地，交通的便利吸引着不少欧美侨民和本地富商聚居东山。民国年间，军政要人的别墅在东山更是鳞次栉比。因此，不少广州人认为东山是权贵聚居之地，是“贵气”的所在。“东山少爷”因而被谈论了近百年。“有权有势住东山”，曾经是一种民俗的心理认同。

20 世纪 20 年代初欧美传教士陆续在东山兴建教堂，创办了教会学校和慈善机构。

European and American missioners began to build churches in Dongshan in early 1920's and set up religious schools and charity organizations.

20世纪30年代初的东山梅花村，因曾遍植梅花，而博得这一雅名。以陈济棠别墅为代表，中西合璧的建筑格调，如今还能寻访历历旧痕。这一批掩映在绿树中的别墅有着欧洲别墅的“乡间风格”，质朴、宁静、休闲。

The Meihua (Plum) Village of Dongshan got this name because lots of plum trees were planted here in early 1930's. We still vaguely see the vestige of history here from this typical villa which was once owned by Chen Jitang and had a mixture of eastern and western construction style.Surrounded by green trees, these villas had the simple, quiet and relaxing flavors of European countryside.

1930年寺贝通津的新式住宅。当时东山已是享誉一时的高尚住宅区。

The fashionable houses at Sibeitongjin in 1930. Dongshan was a famous high class residenfial area at that time.

◎沙面　Shamian Island

“白鹅潭水水连天，望入城中象万千”，“向晚棹花春浪软，香云先渡白鹅潭”。这些诗句所描摹的白鹅潭乃与市区西南面的沙面相连，水木清华、风月无边。清咸丰十一年（1861 年），英、法两国从清政府手中租借沙面建立租界后便挖河筑堤，把它从珠江北岸强行切出，造就了一个南临珠江，东、西、北三面河涌环绕的 22 万平方米的椭圆形小岛。这里有独立的发电厂、供水系统、电报局、码头、银行、洋行、医院、教堂等。沙面作为英法租界的 80 多年历史，诚然是一段主权受辱的记载。但它在广州近代史的进程中，却客观地推进了广州城市化的步伐。

清同治四年（1865 年）的沙面租界。

The Shamian Concession in the 4th year of Emperor Tongzhi of the Qing Dynasty (in 1865).

20 世纪 30 年代初沙面鸟瞰。

A bird's-eye view of Shamian in early 1930's.

20 世纪 30 年代沙面的古树与江景。一个半世纪过去了，沙面躲过了一场场天灾人祸，近百棵百年以上树龄的古木仍然盘根错节。

The old trees and river scene of Shamian in 1930's. In the last one and a half century, Shamian avoided thousands of disasters. Here, dozens of 100-year-old trees are still growing luxuriantly nowadays.

沙面的教堂建筑。150多座西式建筑遍布全岛，从新古典主义、浪漫主义、折衷主义到“一战”后影响最大的现代主义，林林总总，堪称19世纪60年代至20世纪40年代西方建筑风格的博览会。

The churches in Shamian. On this island, there are western style buildings of all kinds, including the new classicism, romanticism, "compromism", as well as the most influential school after the First World War — the modernism, which seem to be a western style, as well as construction fair from 1860's to 1940's.

◎永汉路 Yonghan Road

这条路在清代由南至北依次称永清街、雄镇直街、双门底和承宣直街，是由珠江上岸进入广州城的官道。新任总督、巡抚都少不了在“官用码头”天字码头乘舆张盖，经过这条路抵达位于越华路的两广总督署。1918年，广州南关发生火灾，当局拆除永汉门扩修马路；1919年为纪念汉人再坐江山，改原来的“永清”为“永汉”，20世纪60年代改为北京路。这里一直就是广州城内的商业中心和文化中心，名店林立，九同章、三多轩、陈李济都是广州的百年骄傲。

“珠宝奇珍列万般，书坊画店任盘桓。怡情争说双门底，不让京都大栅栏。”昔日的双门底以书坊、古董街和花市为人所熟识。图中民国初年的双门底，确实招幌如林。

Shuangmendi was once well known for its book stores, antique streets and flower market. People said that Shuangmendi was even more famous than Dashanlan in the capital because of the jewelry shops, bookshops and painting shops here. This picture shows the thousands of shop signs in Shuangmendi in the early period of the China Republic.

1920 年扩建的永汉路。

The expasion of Yonghan Road in 1920.

20世纪20年代末的永汉路“骑楼”如廊。该路是广州最早兴建“骑楼”的马路之一。

There were so many “arcade buildings” in Yonghan Road in late 1920's, which is one of the streets where such “arcade buildings” were built at the earliest developing stage in Guangzhou.

20 世纪 30 年代初为纪念国民党元老胡汉民，永汉路曾改称汉民路。

In early 1930's, Yonghan Road was renamed Hanmin Road in order to commemorate the senior KMT member Hu Hanmin.

1966 年永汉路更名为北京路。典型的“方盒子”楼宇和被广州人称为“火柴盒”的新型公共汽车，充溢着那个时代的气息。

In 1966, Yonghan Road was again renamed Beijing Road. Both the typical “square boxes” of buildings and the new buses that the local people called “match boxes” here give the typical flavors of that time.

◎惠爱路 Huiai Road

惠爱路为清代广州城横贯东西两城门的主要街道，也是出入布政司、巡抚部院、广东都司等官署的必经之路。清代和民国初年称惠爱街。1918—1919年在广州的道路改建中，建成惠爱东、中、西路。1948年，为纪念孙中山而改名中山路。今天仍为广州市区主要的交通干线，沿路是广州重要的商业区。

20世纪20年代的惠爱路。在这条路上，曾经有大新公司、艳芳照相馆、惠如楼、新华电影院、菜根香素食馆、妙奇香茶楼、致美斋等百年老号，它们在20世纪90年代的地铁建设中几乎集体消失。

Huiai Road in 1920's. Here, there were once lots of 100-year-old shops and restaurants, such as the Daxin Company, the Yanfang photoshop, the Huiru Building, the Xinhua Cinema, the Caigenxiang Vegetarian Restaurant, the Miaoqixiang Tea House and the Zhimeizhai Store, etc.But they almost all disappeared because of the subway constructions in 1990's.

20 世纪 40 年代初的惠爱路。

Huiai Road in early 1940's.

新中国成立后，原惠爱东、中、西路分别改为中山四、五、六路。20 世纪五六十年代，中山路不仅是广州重要的商业区，而且还是政治宣传的舞台。图为 50 年代行进在中山路的游行队伍。

Huiaidong Road, Huiaizhong Road and Huiaixi Road were respectively renamed Zhongshansi Road, Zhongshan-wu Road and Zhongshanliu Road after new China was set up. In 1950's and 1960's, Zhongshan Road was not only an important CBD but also a stage of political publicity in Guangzhou. The picture shows the parade in Zhongshan Road in 1950's.

◎越华路 Yuehua Road

越华路东连仓边路，西接吉祥路，长577米，宽13米。清代因地处广东布政司（今省财政厅）后边而称司后街。清咸丰十年（1860年）劳崇光迁两广总督署至司后街的华宁里口（今省民政厅）。1920年扩建为马路，因街内有清代越华书院，改名越华路。

民国初年司后街残墙败瓦。

The broken walls and tiles at Sihou Street in the early period of the Republic of China.

1911 年 4 月 27 日，黄兴发动黄花岗起义，率领“选锋队”从司后街小东营起义指挥部出发，攻打两广总督署。广东光复后，军政府接收原两广总督署，这里便成了民国广东省政府的所在地。图为 20 世纪 30 年代越华路上的广东省政府。

On April 27, 1911, Huang Xing started the Huanghuagang Uprising. Setting off from the Xiaodongying Uprising Headquarter at Sihou Street, he lead his pioneers to attack the Guangdong-Guangxi Governor's Office. After recovering Guangdong, the military government took over the Governor's Office and turned it into the Guangdong Government Deparment of the Republic of China.This picture shows the Guangdong Government Department in Yuehua Road in 1930's.

◎白云路 Baiyun Road

1921 年建成的白云路曾经是广州道路建设的典范，有“模范马路”之称。该路路面很宽，并有着复式路线，起止于广九站和川龙桥，长 610 余米，宽 50 米，路口设广九铁路火车站，规划和建筑堪称一流。20 世纪 20 年代鲁迅执教中山大学时，曾居住在白云路面向东濠涌的白云楼。

20 世纪 20 年代的白云路，十分疏朗开阔。

The wide Baiyun Road in 1920's.

可能因为考虑到火车站的特殊功能，当年的白云路有着宽阔的路面和整齐的绿化带。

The Baiyun Road was built wide and with tidy treelawns probably because of the special transportation functions of the train station there.

◎小北路 Xiaobei Road

小北路从前是市民游白云山的必经之路，所以又有“登峰路”的乡野之名。而它的正名是因傍依清代广州城小北门而得。清代称小北直街，1927 年扩建成马路，路长 1023 米，宽 13～20 米。

小北路在 1927 年扩建前是通往白云山的幽静的郊野小道。1928 年，广州商会会长邹殿邦在此创办著名的北园酒家，正是以乡野风格取胜，有“山前酒肆，水尾茶寮”之称。图为扩建中的小北路。

The Xiaobei Road used to be a quiet suburban path leading to the Baiyun Mountain before being enlarged in 1927. In 1928, Zou Dianbang, Chairman of the Guangzhou Commercial Organization, established the well-known Beiyuan Restaurant here which was famous for its country flavor and the laudatory title of “Restaurant in front of the mountain and beside the river.” The picture shows the Xiaobei Road which was then being enlarged.

1927 年扩建的小北路。

The enlarged Xiaobei Road in 1927.

◎四牌楼　The Four Memorial Stone Archways

广州的四牌楼指的是明朝惠爱坊、忠贤坊、孝友坊和贞烈坊，立于广州城南北走向的四牌楼街上，街名由此而得。清代，因明朝四牌楼被毁而在该街重修康熙朝人瑞坊、总揆百僚坊、戊辰进士坊和乙丑进士坊。同治年间，仓边街的盛世直臣坊也被移至四牌楼街。清代的四牌楼周围热闹非凡，形成了“四牌楼市”，其中以春节到上元节的“灯市”为最盛，时任两广总督的阮元有《羊城灯市》诗：“海鳖云凤巧玲珑，归德门前列彩屏。市火蛮宾余物力，丰年羊穗复仙灵。月能彻夜春光满，人似探花马未停。见说瀛洲双客到，书窗更有万灯青。”而《羊城竹枝词》描绘的盛况是“节近元宵乐未休，买灯花到四牌楼。愿郎卖

1930 年四牌楼扩建成长 554 米、宽 16 米的中华中路。

In 1930, the Four Memorial Stone Archways was enlarged and renamed Zhonghuazhong Road, which was 554 metres long and 16 metres wide.

得灯花后，照妾青春到白头。”1930 年，该街拓宽成中华中路。1947 年牌坊被拆迁，其中康熙朝人瑞坊、戊辰进士坊移至粤秀山百步梯，总揆百僚坊、盛世直臣坊移至汉民公园（现为南越国宫署遗址考古挖掘工地），乙丑进士坊移至岭南大学。1954 年，为纪念广州解放，该路又更名解放中路。“文化大革命”期间，迁走的五座牌坊在劫难逃，越秀山脚的两座牌坊被砸碎，其余三座牌坊也被拆毁。1999 年 11 月，“乙丑进士坊”在中山大学修复落成。

20 世纪 30 年代初的中华中路。
Zhonghuazhong Road in early 1930's.

20世纪30年代初的四牌楼，从南而北立于通衢大道上，以石柱、石梁、石幔、石匾、门前石辘座等预制凿刻件叠架而成，飞檐高翘，有题刻的横石匾。中间较宽高的石门可通车。两旁是人行的矮小侧门。

The Four Memorial Stone Archways in early 1930's. It was built north and south trend in the thoroughfare Avenue by using prefabricated and carved components of stone columns, stone beams, stone curtains, stone plaques and gate windlasses. The horizontal stone plaque was nicely carved and set off by the high eaves. The tall stone gate in the centre was designed to let vehicles pass while the shorter ones on both sides were for pedestrians.

◎大新路　Daxin Road

大新路在古时是城南的护城濠，北有玉带河，南临珠江。明时因集散山货、茶叶而称山茶巷。明末因是广州“新城”新建的大街而改称大新街。1931 年拆建成马路才易名大新路，长 1106 米，宽 11 米。沿路云集象牙雕刻、珠宝玉器、瓷像、乐器、狮鼓等传统商行。乾隆举人叶詹岩流寓粤东时有《广州杂咏》百首，其中有咏大新街繁华的：“珍奇多聚大新街，翡翠明珠次第排。买得玉鱼归未晚，双门才挂午时牌。”

清末的大新街，六排长石铺设，人流如织。从前连孩童也懂得它的热闹：“阿姑乖，嫁后街。后街有嘢卖，后街有鲜鱼鲜肉卖，又有鲜花戴。戴唔晒，栖落床头被老鼠拉。拉去边，拉去大新街。”

Daxin Street in the late Qing Dynasty was a busy street. Its ground was laid across by 6 pieces of stone. Even kids knew her prosperity by chanting “My fair aunty, please marry nowhere but the backstreet, for there are lots of things sold there, fish and meat and pretty flowers. So many flowers keep dropping to your bedside. And even mice carry them to sell, Where? to Daxin Street, of course!”

从小街变成通衢大道，多了高楼，少了人气。图为1931年修成通车的大新路。

From a small street to a wide road, Daxin Road was enlarged and open to traffic in 1931, with more tall buildings but fewer visitors.

◎长堤　The Changdi

长堤习惯上指东起五仙路口，西接仁济路一段。清初时还是珠江的河道，至清末形成陆地。清光绪十五年（1889 年）两广总督张之洞修筑南关至天字码头段的珠江堤岸马路。光绪二十九年（1903 年）岑春煊督粤后，设堤工局，续修堤岸马路，至清宣统二年（1910 年）修成长堤马路川龙口至西濠口段。1920 年进行扩建，取名长堤大马路，全长 710 米，宽 11.5 米，为市区繁华商业区，先施公司、爱群大厦、东亚酒店、大三元酒家等商贸大厦和酒店林立，被誉为广州的“外滩”。

20 世纪 20 年代初的这一幅长堤街景，似乎就是从旧电影中直接剪裁下来的镜头。

Changdi Street in early 1920’s seems to be a close-up directly cut from an old movie.

30 年代初广州长堤全景。

A full view of Guangzhou along Changdi in early 1930's.

↑先施公司
↑海珠公园
↑（背景）白云山
↑电灯公司

20世纪30年代末40年代初的长堤街景。

A scene of Changdi Street from late 1930's to early 1940's.

◎西堤　The Xidi

东接长堤，西连沙基的西堤也是临江的繁华商业区，集中了广州最具欧美风情的建筑。这里直到清代仍然是珠江的河岸浅滩，1914 年才修筑成西堤马路。1926 年 3 月起扩建，称西堤大马路。1981 年改名为沿江西路，长 1670 米，宽 11～20 米。

20 世纪 30 年代初繁华的西堤，集中了广州的众多之最：最早的百货公司；最高的钢筋混凝土大厦；最洪亮的大钟。名闻一时的大新公司、爱群大厦、大三元酒家、中央大酒店、广州海关，是了解广州近代商业历史不可或缺的实证材料。

There were lots of Guangzhou's "mosts" here at this busiest Xidi Street in early 1930's in Guangzhou——the earliest department store, the tallest building of reinforced concerete, and the loudest and clearest clock, together with the Daxin Company, the Aiqun Mansion, the Dasanyuan Restaurant, the Central Hotel and the Guangzhou Customhouse——all these are valuable and substantial evidence in learning and understanding Guangzhou modern commercial history.

1954 年的西堤大马路上，行进的游行队伍。

The Parade in Xidi Street in 1954.

◎太平南路　Taipingnan Road

太平南路是 1919 年广州拆鸡翼城后填平了西濠修筑的，由于位于广州城太平门之南，故名。北接丰宁路（今人民中路），南抵珠江。长 820 米，宽 32 米，为当时广州最宽的马路之一。沿路是新亚大酒店、中央大酒店、冯强鞋店等盛极一时的名号。1966 年改名人民南路。

20 世纪 30 年代初的太平南路，两旁高敞的骑楼建筑和悠闲的行人，颇有步行街的意味。

Taipingnan Road in the early 1930's. Both the tall and wide arcaded building and the relaxed pedestrinas here show the flavor of a modern vehicle-free shopping street.

20世纪40年代的太平南路。

Taipingnan Road in 1940's.

◎六二三路 Liuersan Road

“六二三路”位于沙面北面，原称沙基大街，商业繁盛，仓库、钱庄、旅馆楼宇林立，花筵酒家乘时而兴。20 世纪 20 年代早期，开辟马路仅到沙面西桥谷埠附近，四乡的谷物要靠木船沿珠江运到沙基涌，依靠人力搬进谷仓，造就了这一带旺盛的人气。

1925 年 6 月 23 日发生“沙基惨案”，事后广东革命政府为纪念惨案中的死难者而改路名为六二三路。同年底进行扩建。沿街原为商业区，20 世纪 50 年代起渐为民宅。

清末的沙基大街。沙基涌上舟楫林立，可以想见当日水运的繁忙。

Shaji Street in the late Qing Dynasty. There were so many boats here in the Shaji River that one can imagine how busy the shipment was at that time.

1925年6月23日，香港、广州工人和各界群众10万多人在沙基游行，支援上海“五卅”运动。遭到沙面租界的英法军警的袭击，造成死伤严重的“沙基惨案”。后在此地竖立“毋忘此日”碑以纪念，路名由此而改为六二三路。

On June 23, 1925, over 100 thousand demonstrators, induding workers from Hong Kong and Guangzhou and people from all fields, held a demonstration in Shaji Street in order to support the May 30th Movement in Shanghai. The parade was attacked by the British and French armed Police in the Shamian Concession, which caused lots of injuries and death and was known as the Shaji Massacre. A Monument of "Never Forget This Day" was erected right here to commemorate this march.And the street was renamed Liuersan (June 23) Road.

20世纪30年代的六二三路。骑楼与疍船，正是旧日广州别具一格的标识。

Liuersan Road in 1930's. Both the arcaded buildings and wooden boat were typical signs of old Guangzhou.

◎十三行路 Shisanhang Road

十三行路东起人民南路，西至杉木栏路。1924年修建，长315米，宽12米。因清代这里曾有著名的十三行，故名。十三行是清政府为了保障行商对贸易的垄断，便利对外贸的约束和关税的征收而设立的商行，清康熙二十五年（1686年）始设。其中既有十三行商从事贸易的行号，又有供外商居停的商馆。清道光二十三年（1843年）中英《南京条约》签订后，其外贸特权被取消，乃趋没落。

清道光二十四年（1844年）的广州十三行商馆。屈大均的《广东新语》形容十三行之盛是："洋船争出是官商，十字门开向二洋。五丝八丝广缎好，银钱堆满十三行。"

The Guangzhou Shisanhang Commercial Guild in the 24th year of Emperor Daoguang (in 1844). Qu Dajun described the prosperity of Shisanhang in his *New Descriptions of Guangdong* in this way ——"When Guangzhou opens to the outside world, official businessmen trade with foreign countries.Guangdong has been famous for its silk and textile, and all money goes to Shisanhang."

1924 年建成的十三行路。

Shisanhang Road in 1924.

1922 年的十三行街。

Shisanhang Street in 1922.

20世纪30年代十三行路与太平南路交界处。

The juncture of Shisanhang Road and Taipingnan Road in 1930's.

◎靖远路　Jingyuan Street

靖远路北至十三行路，南抵西堤，1924年修建，长369米，宽12米。清代为十三行商馆的中心地带，西方人称为旧中国街。20世纪50年代修建广州文化公园时被分为南北两段。1981年定名靖远北路。

这一幅外销画表现的是19世纪30年代十三行靖远街街景：整齐划一的商馆，街上的行人中西杂处。

This picture which was once sold abroad tells the scene of Jingyuan Lane of Shisanhang Street in 1830's——the tidy commercial guilds and both Chinese and foreign pedestrians.

19世纪50年代的十三行靖远街口。

Jingyuan Lane of Shisanhang Street in 1850's.

1924年修成的靖远路。

Jingyuan Road was built in 1924.

◎上下九　Shangxiajiu Street

上下九由上九路和下九路组成，东起人民南路，西抵文昌南路口与第十甫相接。原为西关上九甫和下九甫，1918 年扩建成路，旧称为上九甫路、下九甫路，共长 747 米，宽 17 米。明末清初以来，上下九一直是广州的商业中心之一，金银首饰、百货、服装、鞋帽、布料、药材、饮食等商铺云集，如今仍是广州繁华的商业步行街。

1929 年上下九铺设沥青路的情形。

Shangxiajiu Street was being leveled with bitumen in 1929.

1929年整修后的上下九街景。商业街是靠名店品牌修筑的，一路延伸的皇上皇腊味店、纶章纺织品商店、广州酒家、清平饭店、陶陶居、莲香楼等，营造了这条商业街货如轮转的氛围。

Shangxiajiu Street in 1929 after being rebuilt.This prosperous shopping street was full of famous shops and restaurants such as the Huang-shanghuang Cured Bacon Shop, the Lunzhang Textile Shop, the Guangzhou Restaurant, the Qingping Restaurant, the Taotaoju Restaurant and the Lianxianglou Restaurant.

◎桨栏路　Jianglan Street

桨栏路东起光复路，西至杨巷路、长乐路交会处，与十八甫路相连。1928 年起扩街修路，1931 年完工，长 302 米，宽 12.5 米。旧书记载道：“羊城呼市为栏，如竹栏、果栏之类。”清屈大均的《广东新语》解释道：“广州凡食物所聚皆曰栏。贩者从栏中买取，乃以鬻诸城内外之称，惟两粤有之。粤东之栏以居物，粤西之栏以居人。”桨栏路也是因原街为船桨集市，故名。谭敬昭《听云楼诗草·珠江柳枝词》“豆栏东接井栏西”句自注云：“豆栏、井栏，并街名，当为桨栏之转。”

民国初年的桨栏街。招幌林立，一派传统商业街市的风情。

Jianglan Street in the early period of the Republic of China. All the signboards gave a flavor of a Chinese traditional shopping street.

20世纪30年代初扩建的桨栏路。商铺点缀着西化的阳台和栏杆。

Jianglan Road was enlarged in early 1930's. All the shops here were ornamented with western style corridors and handrails.

◎南华路 Nanhua Street

南华路东起海珠桥下芳草围西侧，西抵洪德路。南华西路至同福西路以南一带是十三行行商潘家、伍家和张家家园。1926年拆龙溪西约、中约、福麟街、紫来街、冼涌、跃龙东街等建成，长2300米，宽11米，分东、中、西三段。因地处河南，并祈繁华发达之意，故名。这里是河南主要的商业、交通要道。

20世纪40年代初的南华东路。它是河南骑楼建筑比较集中的马路。

Nanhuadong Street in early 1940's. Lots of arch buildings were built here on the south of the Pearl River.

◎同福大街和同福路 Tongfu Street &Tongfu Road

同福大街和同福路地处广州河南，因原属广州佛教“五大丛林”之一的“海幢寺”为佛门福地而名。同福大街南接同福中路，北连南华中路。20 世纪初建街，长 172 米，宽 3.5 米。同福路则修建于 1926 年，全长 2750 米，宽 18 米，分东、中、西三段，因在同福大街旁而得名，为河南主要的商业、交通要道。

20 世纪 20 年代末的同福路。在这一条街上曾经有伍家花园、海幢寺、潘家寺、海福寺。

Tongfu Street in late 1920's. There used to be some Buddha temples here, such as the Wujia Garden, the Haizhuang Temple, the Panjia Temple and the Haifu Temple.

20世纪40年代初的同福西路。

Tongfuxi Road in early 1940's.

◎中山公路 Zhongshan Highway

中山公路东起黄埔港，西至冼村与黄埔大道相交。1925 年底省港罢工委员会为实施孙中山的《建国方略》，发动 3000 多名群众修建，次年春建成，全长约 13 公里，宽 11 米，为纪念孙中山而名中山公路。1987 年扩建为 48 米宽的混凝土路，改名中山大道，是沟通市区和黄埔港的交通要道，也是市区东部的主要出口之一。

20 世纪 60 年代的中山公路。
Zhongshan Highway in 1960's.

20 世纪 30 年代初的中山公路。
Zhongshan Highway in early 1930's.

2【名胜古迹】

名胜是古城的家珍。那些古朴精致的台殿楼阁，那些华美别致的近代建筑，都结合了自然的灵秀与人文的意象，一起构成羊城最堪寻味的经典，诠释着这个城市兼容并蓄的品格。

◎白云山 The Baiyun Mountain

白云山位于广州市北郊，是五岭之一大庾岭的余脉，由30多个山峰连绵组成，总面积28平方公里，大致呈东北西南走向。因山峰顶常有白云飘绕而得名。主峰摩星岭海拔高度为382.4米，古称“天南第一峰”。白云山自古是广州著名的游览胜地，留下众多骚人墨客的题咏，也留下了安期飞仙、九龙等神话传说。“蒲涧濂泉”、“白云晚望”、“景泰僧归”、“云山锦绣”、“云山叠翠”等景致分别入选历代羊城八景，是广州人听涛观云的胜处。现存有九龙泉、天南第一峰、能仁寺、“虎”字石刻、滴水岩、蒲涧等古迹，新辟有明珠楼、水月阁、白云松涛、白云晓望、鸣春谷等景点。

1908年，从白云山顶往北望，只见满山遍野的坟茔。

In 1908, looking towards north from the peak of Baiyun Mountain, the mountain was covered with mounds.

20世纪20年代修建的白云山环山公路。

The Baiyun Mountain Circus Highway was built in 1920's.

枝柯蔽天、平石如磴的白云山登山石阶。

The tree-covered climbing stairs are all built of big pieces of rock.

20世纪30年代掩映在绿丛深处的白云山能仁寺。

The Nengren Temple was among big green trees in 1930's.

◎镇海楼 Zhenhai Tower

镇海楼在越秀山上，据说明洪武初年，越秀山上有紫云黄气升腾，传云为王者之气，永嘉侯朱亮祖是以建楼镇之，曰镇海楼。在此处登楼望远，有江水浩渺的胜概，故有“望海楼”之称；又因楼高五层，民间俗称五层楼。其后四五百年间屡损屡修，1928年重修时，把原来楼内木结构改为钢筋混凝土结构，但明代砌筑的城墙仍存。1929年改为广州市市立博物院。1950年易名广州博物馆。镇海楼以瑰丽雄伟的明代建筑风格，先后以“镇海层楼”和“越秀层楼”列清代和现代羊城八景之一，并留下无数文人骚客的题咏。

清末民初的镇海楼，危居越秀山的小蟠龙岗上，一楼独秀，明代的城墙蜿蜒可见。清末彭玉麟所撰写的楹联“万千劫危楼尚存，问谁摘斗摩霄，目空今古;五百年故侯安在，使我倚栏看剑，泪洒英雄。”至今仍脍炙人口。

The elegant Zhenhai Building, which was built on the Xiaopanlong Hillock during the late Qing Dynasty and the early period of the Republic of China, overlooks all other hills and the nearby city wall built in the Ming Dynasty. The couplet on this building written by Peng Yulin during the late Qing Dynasty is still widely loved——“Touching the sky and stars, the supercilious building surprisingly survived thousands of disasters. Standing by the rails, I cherish the memory of the heroes as I seem to clearly see the battlefront 500 years ago.”

1908 年，远眺越秀山上的镇海楼和观音寺，图正中前部是一个清真先贤古墓。

Zhenhai Five-storey Building and Kuan-yin Temple in Yuexiu Mountain in 1908. The mausoleum of Moslem Masters in the middle of the forepart of the picture.

20世纪30年代易名为市立博物院的镇海楼，一直是广州的标志性建筑之一。

The Zhenhai Building, which was renamed the Municipal Museum in 1930's, has been the symbolic building of Guangzhou.

20世纪40年代初的镇海楼。

The Zhenhai Building in early 1940's.

◎番禺学宫　Confucian Panyu Academy

位于中山四路的番禺学宫建于明洪武三年（1370年），清乾隆、光绪年间重修。学宫原来有广三路，深五进的宏大规模。今中路建筑仅存棂星门、泮池拱桥、大成门、大成殿、崇圣殿和东西廊庑；左路建筑尚存明伦堂、光霁堂、头门、八桂儒林门；右路仅存头门。清末废除科举后，这里改为番禺公立中学，民国初年又改为私立八桂中学。1926年，毛泽东在此举办第六期农民运动讲习所。1950年，禺山中学和八桂中学在该处合并为番禺中学。1953年开辟为农民运动讲习所旧址纪念馆。

清末的番禺学宫。它是番禺县学和文庙，每年农历二月八日举行祭孔典礼。

The Panyu Academy in the late Qing Dynasty, which is Urban School and Confucian Temple in Panyu, held a confucious memorial ceremony on Feb.8 every lunar year.

20世纪50年代的农讲所纪念馆。新中国成立后，“番禺学宫”已被“农讲所”这一名称所代替，成为广州市的中小学生接受爱国主义教育的胜地，也是观光客流连之所。

The Memorial Hall of the Peasants' Movement Academy in 1950's. After new China was founded, the Panyu Academy was renamed the Peasants' Movement Academy, and became a place for students to get patriotic education, and a place for tourism as well.

1950年的番禺中学。

The Panyu Middle School in 1950.

◎光孝寺 The Guangxiao Temple

“未有广州，先有光孝”，可见光孝寺渊源悠久。光孝寺的寺址原为南越王赵建德的王府，三国时，东吴骑都尉虞翻谪徙居此讲学，庭园中遍植苛子树，因名虞苑，亦称苛林。虞翻身后，其舍宅始辟为佛寺，称为制止寺。后寺名多番更改，至南宋绍兴二十一年（1151年），改称报恩光孝禅寺，苛林易名诃

光孝寺的大雄宝殿，始建于东晋，清顺治十一年（1654年）改建。“尘机方外息，幽趣静中坐”，为明代孙贲对光孝寺的吟咏。

The Daxiong Hall of the Guangxiao Temple was built in the Dongjin Dynasty and rebuilt in 1654 (the 11th year of Emperor Shunzhi of the Qing Dynasty.) In the Ming Dynasty, Sun Ben described the Guangxiao Temple vividly in his verse——“The temple, resting itself in dust, situates tranquilly among trees.”

林。它是岭南佛寺中历史最久、规模最大的寺院，为广州佛教“五大丛林”之首。天王殿旧日楹联云：“禅教遍寰中，兹为最初福地；祗园开岭表，此是第一名山。”禅宗六祖惠能曾在古菩提树下祝发受戒。树西有瘗发塔，藏有六祖头发。“光孝菩提”也由此成为宋代羊城八景之一。光孝寺亦是历代中外高僧传教译经，进行佛教文化交流的中心。达摩、惠能、义净、不空、鉴真等先后在此驻足，弘扬佛法。现寺内保存有大雄宝殿、瘗发塔、六祖殿、达摩井、睡佛楼等古建筑以及东西铁塔、大悲幢及大批碑刻等，都是珍贵的佛教遗迹。

为纪念惠能在光孝寺削发受戒而建造的瘗发塔。八面七层发塔，仿楼阁式样，各面都雕有佛像。

This Tower was built to memorize Master Huineng who was initiated into monkhood in the Guangxiao Temple.The tower, inmitating the attic style, has 8 sides and 7 storeys, with Statues of Buddha in every side.

◎六榕寺　The Liurong Temple

六榕寺位于六榕路，始创于南朝刘宋年间，初名宝庄严寺。南汉末毁于火，北宋端拱二年（989 年）重建，改名净慧寺。北宋元符三年（1100 年），苏轼来寺游览，见寺内环植六株榕树，遂书题“六榕”两字，寺僧为榜，悬于山门。清光绪元年（1875 年），寺院重修后，易名六榕寺。寺内最著者为花塔，“巍峨轮奂，雄耸天半，海舶收港，引为表望”，原建于梁大同三年（537 年），内藏梁武帝母舅昙裕法师从印度带回的舍利子。唐代文学家王勃游经此处，撰写了《广州宝庄严寺舍利塔碑》一文。后塔与寺俱毁于火。宋绍圣四年（1097 年）重修寺塔，更名千佛塔。1935 年再次修葺后，因塔身色彩斑斓而称花塔。花塔为砖木结构，高 57.6 米，登塔可俯瞰羊城风光。

20 世纪 20 年代末六榕寺远景。

The Liurong Temple in the late 1920's.

1928年的六榕寺花塔。塔刹用的是铜柱，铸于元代，柱身上密布着1023尊浮雕小佛像以及云彩缭绕的天宫宝塔图。

The Flower Tower in the Liurong Temple in 1928. The copper pillars of the tower were casted in the Yuan Dynasty. On the pillars there was a relief sculpture of 1023 small statues of Buddha and heaven towers in colorful clouds.

六祖惠能铜像，铸造于北宋端拱二年（989年）。

The copper statue of the 6th Founder, Master Huineng, was casted in 989 (the 2nd year of Emperor Duangong in the Beisong Dynasty).

六榕寺正门上的对联：“一塔有碑留博士，六榕无树记东坡。”博士指初唐四杰之首王勃，其时他往交趾省亲，途经广府，撰有《广州宝庄严寺舍利塔碑》，长3200多字，为全国佛塔碑文之冠。

There is a couplet at the front gate of the Liurong Temple——“On the tower, the stone inscription reminds people of the Doctor, while inside the temple, there are no trees in memory of the great poet Dongpo.” The Doctor refers to Wang Bo, the first of the 4 most outstanding poets of the early Tang Dynasty.At that time, he was on his way to Jiaozhi to visit his relatives and stopped in Guangzhou, and wrote *The Pagoda Inscription of Guangzhou Baozhuangyan Temple*, which has as many as 3200 characters, and is regarded as the longest inscription among Buddhas pagodas.

◎华林寺 The Hualin Temple

华林寺位于下九路。此地古时是海岸。梁大通元年（527年），西竺高僧达摩泛海至广州，在此处登岸。后人在达摩登岸处建庵纪念，称西来庵，该地因此称西来初地。清顺治十一年（1654年），宗符禅师募捐扩建西来庵，改名华林寺。寺内禅房、僧舍具备，并建有大雄宝殿、达摩堂、祇树园等，成为广州佛教“五大丛林”之一。清康熙四十年（1701年），寺内增建舍殿，内供有舍利塔，塔基藏有祖师舍利。华林寺最有名的是它的五百罗汉堂。清道光二十六年（1846年），主持祇园和尚奉诏始建五百罗汉堂，除供奉释迦牟尼佛、阿弥陀佛和弥勒佛外，在廊两侧排列着神态各异的五百尊罗汉像，罗汉堂中央还有一铜铸阿育王塔。1923年，市政厅为筹集北伐军费将华林寺拍卖，寺舍大部分被拆毁。“文化大革命”期间，五百罗汉像又被捣毁。20世纪90年代后期复建五百罗汉堂。

20世纪20年代罗汉堂的布局呈“田字形”，四个天井采光，使回廊明亮疏朗，五百罗汉像是寺僧祇园至杭州净慈寺描图而仿塑的，塑像之一是意大利旅行家马可·波罗像。“共向华林种福田，痴情儿女最堪怜；低头五百阿罗汉，一个心香乞一年。”五百罗汉曾寄寓了人间多少祈福的企盼。

The Arhat Hall in 1920's was built in the shape a square, with four lighting yards which made the winding corridor spacy and bright. The 500 arhat statues here were built by exactly imitating the figures which were traced by Monk Zhi Yuan who went to the Jingci Temple in Hangzhou.One of the statues is the ltalian Traveler, Marco Polo. The 500 arhat figures have been representing people's pray and hope for peace and happiness.

六面七级，造型华丽、雕刻精美的舍利塔，为星岩白石所造，塔基中有密封的石、铜、银、木质小盒，石函盖上有“舍利子”三个大朱字。

The elegant Buddhist Pagoda, which is delicately carved and has 6 sides and 7 storeys, is made of white star rock. lnside the base, there are stone, copper, silver and wooden boxes which are all sealed up. The name “Buddhist Pagoda” is carved on the top of the stone culvert in red color.

◎大佛寺 The Dafo Temple

大佛寺位于惠福东路惠新中街。原址为南汉的新藏寺，元代建为福田庵，明代扩建为龙藏寺，明末改为巡按御史公署，清初塌毁。清顺治年间，平南王尚可喜自捐王俸，安南王捐赠大批楠木，重整寺庙。清康熙二年（1663 年）动工，次年落成。清雍正年间，朝廷向全国佛门颁布谕旨，广州府择大佛寺为宣谕之所，特建宣谕亭。乾隆年间，扩建韦驮、伽蓝二殿和佛境、禅林两座门楼，为广州佛教“五大丛林”之一。林则徐在广州禁烟时，曾设禁烟局于此。1921 年，孙中山为大佛寺成立“佛教阅经社”题赠“阐扬三密”四字。1926 年，周恩来在此举办高级干训班，为北伐培训军政干部。

20 世纪 30 年代初庄严肃穆的大雄宝殿。当时大佛寺规模宏大，曾有头门、钟楼、鼓楼、天王殿、大殿，两侧还有廊庑、方丈、香积厨等房舍。

The Daxiong Hall of the solemn Temple in early 1930's. At that time, the Dafo Temple was built in a broad scale with the Front Gate, the Clock Tower, the Drum Tower, the Supreme Hall, the Grand Hall, and on both sides, the corridor, the abbot's room and the kitchen.

大佛寺内的大佛像。“人过大佛寺，寺佛大过人。”大雄宝殿供奉着释迦牟尼佛、弥勒佛和阿弥陀佛“三宝佛”，均以黄铜制造，高约六米，重十吨，是清康熙二年（1663年）坐镇广州的平南王尚可喜仿京师佛寺修建的。

The Big Buddha Statues in the Dafo Temple.People say, " you go passing the Dafo (Big Buddha) Temple, and all Buddha statues are much bigger than you are! " There are statues of Sakyamuni, Maitreya and Ahmitto in the Daxiong Hall of the temple.All statues are made of bronze, which are 6 metres high and weigh 10 tons each. Shang Kexi, known as King Pingnan and Guangzhou Governor, had the 3 statues built in 1663 (the 2nd year of Emperor Kangxi of the Qing Dynasty) by imitating the Buddha statues in Beijing.

◎海幢寺 The Haizhuang Temple

海幢寺位于同福中路与南华中路间。原址为南汉千秋寺，后废为民居。明代为商人郭龙岳花园，后捐作佛寺，僧人光牟稍加修葺，题额“海幢”。清康熙初年大规模扩建，兴筑大雄宝殿、天王殿、韦驮殿、伽蓝殿、丛观堂、大悲阁、藏经阁等，成为广州佛教“五大丛林”之一。清嘉庆年间，清廷对前来经商的外国商人防范甚严，海幢寺是指定的外商外出游览的两个景点之一，游览时间是每月初八、十八、二十八等三日。1929 年，开辟成河南公园。1933 年易名海幢公园。

画家笔下的清代海幢寺大雄宝殿，原供奉的三宝佛形制宏壮。从画面上的廊柱和雕刻，可见当日的规模。

This is a painting of the Daxiong Hall of Haizhuang Temple in the Qing Dynasty. The three Baddha statues here are grand and tall.From the porch posts and the carving, one can see that the construction scale was rather large at that time.

1908 年，海幢寺内的汉白玉塔。

The tower of Haizhuang Temple in 1908, Which was built with white jade of the Han Dynasty.

20世纪20年代初的海幢寺。民间"未有海幢，先有鹰爪"之说，指明代郭氏花园原植有鹰爪兰。据《羊城古钞》记载："后有鹰爪兰，仍郭园所植。地改而兰仍茂。后郭氏花园入海幢寺，几百年葱茏如昔，夏日兰花怒放，香气满园。"

The Haizhuang Temple in early 1920's. There's a saying——"There are hawk claw orchids in the Garden of Guo's, which later becomes the Haizhuang Temple." And According to the *Yangcheng Old Currency*, "the hawk claw orchids are planted by the people living in the Garden of Guo's in Ming Dynasty. Later, the Garden of Guo's changes into the Haizhuang Temple, and the hawk claw orchids keep growing luxuriantly, giving fragrant in summer days."

20世纪20年代末河南公园的大门。

The Gate of the Henan Park in late 1920's.

◎怀圣寺 Huaisheng Mosque

怀圣寺位于光塔路，是伊斯兰教传入中国后最早的清真寺之一。创建于唐初，相传为阿拉伯传教士阿布·苑葛素所创建。该寺附近是古珠江河畔的蕃坊。寺名“怀圣”，系取怀念圣人穆罕默德之意。因寺内有光塔，故俗称光塔寺。元至正三年（1343 年），寺毁于火，至正十年（1350 年）重建。现存建筑为清康熙三十四年（1695 年）再次修建。寺内有看月楼、长廊、碑亭、经堂、水房、礼拜殿等建筑，兼具中国传统建筑风格和伊斯兰建筑特征。寺门西南角矗立着著名的光塔，为我国目前仅存的唐代伊斯兰教塔。

20 世纪 20 年代怀圣寺的看月楼和光塔。因外表以蚬壳灰批荡，平整光滑，又名“光塔”。原塔顶有金鸡，随风旋转以示风向，可做珠江船只的航海标志。古时每年的五六月间，阿拉伯海船乘季风至广州时，阿拉伯教徒常登塔祈风讯。看月楼位于中轴线上，有四个拱门，红砂岩石墙是典型的重檐歇山顶。画面上的组合体现中西合璧。

The Moon-view Building and the Light Tower of the Huaisheng Mosque in 1920's. The tower, which is plastered by shell lime, is rather neat and smooth, and is also called the “Smooth Tower”. There used to be a “golden cock” on the top of the tower, whose rotation shows the direction of blowing wind that serves as the navigation mark for the sailing boats of the Pearl River. From May to June every year in the ancient times, followers of Arabian Religion would climb the tower to pray for smooth wind as the Arabian boats sailed to Guangzhou in monsoon. The Moon-view Building, which has four arched doors, is right on the central axis. The red sandstone walls are typical construction, and here the Tower and the Building is a good combination of Chinese and Western elements.

有着绿琉璃瓦传统风格的怀圣寺礼拜殿。

The Service Hall of the Huaisheng Mosque, which is built in a traditional way with green colored glaze tiles.

◎石室　The Stone House Catholic Church

石室位于一德路，旧址原是清两广总督署。清咸丰六年（1856年）被英、法侵略军焚毁。后法国租此地兴建教堂，清同治二年（1863年）奠基，光绪四年（1878年）建成。因奠基日为天主教圣心瞻礼节，故名圣心堂。又因全部用花岗岩石砌筑，俗称石室。采用哥特式建筑风格，由法国工程师设计及施工，揭西工匠蔡孝负责工程具体施工。石室坐北向南，东西宽35米，南北深78.79米，地面到塔尖高58.5米，面积2754平方米，为中国现存的最大的石构哥特式建筑。

20世纪30年代初的石室。

The Stone House Catholic Church in early 1930's.

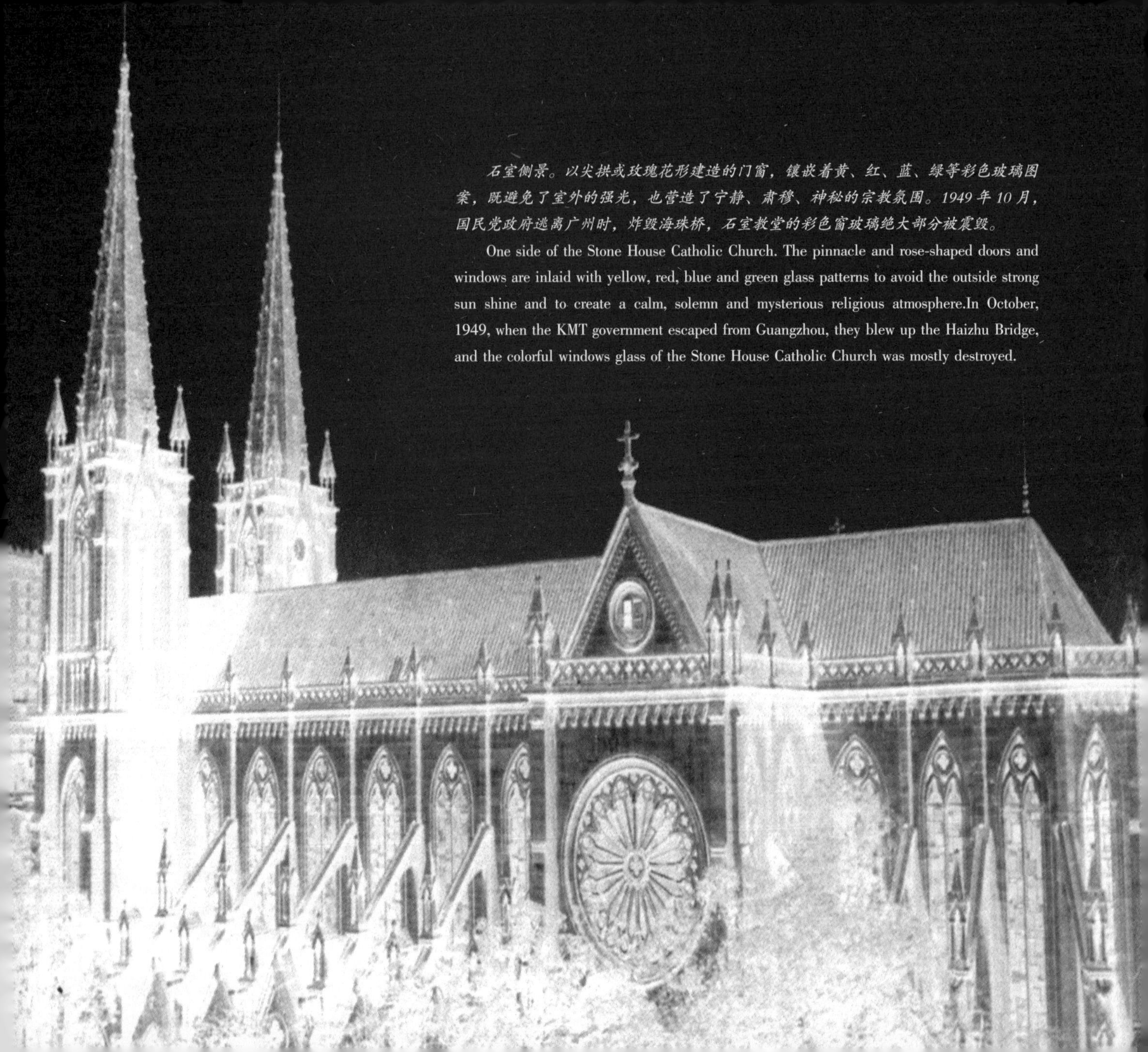

石室侧景。以尖拱或玫瑰花形建造的门窗，镶嵌着黄、红、蓝、绿等彩色玻璃图案，既避免了室外的强光，也营造了宁静、肃穆、神秘的宗教氛围。1949 年 10 月，国民党政府逃离广州时，炸毁海珠桥，石室教堂的彩色窗玻璃绝大部分被震毁。

One side of the Stone House Catholic Church. The pinnacle and rose-shaped doors and windows are inlaid with yellow, red, blue and green glass patterns to avoid the outside strong sun shine and to create a calm, solemn and mysterious religious atmosphere.In October, 1949, when the KMT government escaped from Guangzhou, they blew up the Haizhu Bridge, and the colorful windows glass of the Stone House Catholic Church was mostly destroyed.

◎五仙观 The Wuxian Taoist Temple

五仙观位于惠福西路。相传广州建城之初，曾有五位仙人手持谷穗骑五羊而至，祝这里永无饥荒，后遗谷穗离去，羊即化为石。广州又称羊城、穗城即源于这则神话。五仙观就是祭祀这五仙的谷神庙，宋代建在十贤坊（今北京路财厅前一带）。明洪武十年（1377 年）迁至现址，内有照壁、牌坊、山门、中殿、后殿，两侧有东斋、西斋、三元殿、廊庑等，颇具规模。现存头门、后殿和东斋、西斋部分旧建筑。后殿东侧有坡山古渡遗迹，分别以“穗石洞天”和“五仙霞洞”列入明、清羊城八景。后殿之后，耸立一座建于明洪武七年（1374 年）的大钟楼，号称“岭南第一楼”。1923 年，广州市政厅为筹备军饷，将五仙观拍卖。20 世纪 80 年代后经修葺重新对外开放。

20 世纪 20 年代飞檐斗拱的五仙观牌坊。

The Memorial Arch of the Wuxian Taoist Temple in 1920's.

20世纪30年代初供奉五仙的殿宇。

The Five Celestial Beings are worshiped in the Wuxian Taoist Temple in early 1930's.

岭南第一楼，为明代木构架建筑，上悬一口著名的禁钟。

The first building of Canton, which was built with wooden framwork in Ming Dynasty, a well-known bell hanging on.

◎南海神庙　Nanhai God Temple

南海神庙位于黄埔区庙头，是中国古代著名的海神庙，也是古代海上交通贸易的重要遗址。因庙前有两棵波罗树，故又称波罗庙。南海之帝，在中国的四大海神中地位最显赫。他的职能是“司火兼司水”。隋文帝在开皇十四年（594 年）下诏立祠以祀。此后，历代帝王对南海神都有加冕。唐封为“广利王”，宋加号为“洪圣王”。元诏尊为“广利灵孚王”，明时干脆就称为“南海之神”，清代再封为“南海昭明龙王之神”，民间称为“广利洪圣大王”。古时庙前有码头，海舶进出，按例到庙拜祭，并可在庙旁的扶胥镇交易。以此为起点的古代海上“丝绸之路”通达东南亚、西非和东非，明清时远达欧、美。唐代以后，南海神庙历经扩建

20 世纪 20 年代的南海神庙。每年的农历二月十一至十三的南海神诞，也就是“波罗”诞，曾经是最热闹的庙会。民间俚语“第一游波罗，第二娶老婆”之说，“香火万家市，烟花二月时。居人空巷去，去赛海神祠”便是这庙会的注脚。庙会中出售的“波罗鸡”由于它独有的粘贴制作手法，这就成全了广州人的一句歇后语“波罗鸡——靠黏”，形容一切无赖式的混吃混喝。

The Nanhai God Temple in 1920's. Every lunar year from Feb.11 to 13 is the birthday of the Nanhai Gods, which is also called the Birthday of Boluo.It's the most popular temple fair at that time.Folk sayings describe the temple fair like this——“Going to the fair is far more important than looking for a wife”, and, “Every year in Febuary, burning incense can be smelled every where in the streets.Why are all the houses empty? Because everyone rushes to the temple fair!” People would sell a typical kind of Boluo Chicken during the fair, which was quite sticky because it was cooked in a special way.The Cantonese people have a allegorical saying “the Boluo chicken is famous for being extremely sticky” to describe those who muddle along kidding others.

重修，现占地近3万平方米，内有“海不扬波”石碑坊、头门、仪门、礼亭、大殿和后殿以及唐代至清代古碑等古迹文物。神庙有“岭南碑林”之誉。尚存唐代韩愈碑、宋开宝碑、明太祖御碑等。第三进的礼亭有康熙“万里波澄”御碑。还有东汉的铜鼓、明代铁钟和玉刻南海神印。庙西章丘顶上有浴日亭。“扶胥浴日”是宋、元的羊城八景之一。

南海神庙的内景。

The internal scene of the Nanhai God Temple.

◎荔枝湾 The Litchi Bay

荔枝湾位于今天广州荔湾湖公园一带，唐代由珠江冲积成陆地，地势低平，多池塘洼地。南汉时广种荔枝，因而称“荔枝湾”。这里既有南汉经营的昌华苑、芳华苑、华林园等皇家园林的芳踪，荔红时节的“红云宴”曾是一时之盛，又是元代的御果园，曾有800多棵柠檬树的芳华。由河涌纵横、百舸云集、游人如织构图的“荔湾渔唱”成为明代一帧羊城八景的旧图。清代富商潘仕成的海山仙馆、黄景棠的小画舫斋等分列两岸，更平添几分韵致。这一带存留了老广州对十里荷香、千株荔子的许多记忆，成就了无数人“一枕舢板游河”的消暑凉梦。《羊城竹枝词》：“泮塘夏日荔初红，万树虬珠映水浓。消受绿天亭一角，乱蝉声扬藕花风。”描绘了旧时的水乡风情，艇仔粥、游河、品荔便是荔湾旧事留下来的片段。抗战后，河涌淤积，荔枝湾日渐衰败。1958年在此修建了荔湾湖公园，仍以湖光水色取胜。

20世纪30年代的荔枝湾，游艇如织。

The Litchi Bay with lots of anchored boats.

广州荔枝湾莲池。

The lotus pond of the Litchi Bay.

20世纪30年代的荔枝湾。当年游荔枝湾，多在荔湾涌多宝桥下船。点篙摇橹的女子，戴着极细的银手镯，赤脚穿梭于艇林之间。

The Litchi Bay in 1930's. People at that time often got on board small boats at the Duobao Bridge when touring Litchi Bay. The boat woman, bare foot, and wearing a delicate silver bracelet, is poling the scull.

1953年的荔枝湾风情。

The Litchi Bay in 1953.

◎海山仙馆 Haishan Museum

海山仙馆位于城西荔枝湾，是清代广州规模最大的私家园林，被誉为南粤之冠、人间仙境。清道光年间，由广州富商潘仕成兴建。因门悬对联为两广总督耆英亲书“海上神山，仙人旧馆”，故名海山仙馆。园倚荔枝湾而建，雕镂华丽的亭台楼阁错落其间，山水交融，环绕着游廊曲榭，而沿壁遍嵌的石刻，皆晋、唐以来的名迹，清幽处更添风雅。清同治年间，因园主获罪破产，海山仙馆归官拍卖，终于废没。

清道光二十四年（1844 年）的海山仙馆主楼，有荷风水榭之胜。

The main building of the Haishan Museum in the 24th year of Emperor Daoguang of the Qing Dynasty (in 1844).

海山仙馆的湖上凉亭。潘仕成曾为家园自撰对联：“池馆偶陶情，看此时碧水栏边，那个可人，胜似莲花颜色；乡园重涉趣，悔昔日红尘骑外，几番过客，虚抛荔子光阴。”

The pavilion of Haishan Museum. Pan Shicheng once wrote a couplet for his house: “Stand by the pool, look at clear water, attractive beautiful scenery, cherish the memory of the past.”

海山仙馆主人潘仕成。他原籍福建，生于番禺，以盐商起家，是清朝广州四大富豪之首。原是副贡生，后捐钱买官，得钦赐举人的名衔，官至两广盐运使。他刻有《海山仙馆丛书》、《海山仙馆丛帖》等。

Pan Shicheng, the master of Haishan Museum, whose arcestral home is Fujian, was born in Panyu. He made his fortune from salt trade, and became the chief richer of the four richest of Guangzhou in Qing Dynasty. He was Vice Gongsheng at first and after got a Juren designation by donation and bribery. He was promoted to the official who control salt trade between Guandong and Guangxi. He engraved *Series of Books of Haishan Museum* and *Series* of *Copybooks of Haishan Museum*.

◎陈家祠 The Chenjiaci Ancestral Hall

陈家祠位于今中山七路，为广东全省陈氏合族祠堂，当时又是陈姓子弟温书攻读的地方，所以又称陈氏书院。清光绪十四年（1888年）筹建，二十年（1894年）落成，占地1.32万平方米。陈家祠为“三进三路九堂两厢抄”布局的典型岭南民间宗祠式建筑。建筑宽敞雄伟，结构精练。装饰采用木雕、石雕、砖雕、陶塑、灰塑、铁铸、壁画等广东民间传统建筑工艺。艺术表现题材有历史典故、楼台胜景、吉祥花鸟、岭南风物等，精巧传神，富有浓郁的岭南地方特色，为集广东建筑、装饰工艺之大成的古典建筑。1959年，陈家祠改为广东民间工艺博物馆。2002年以“古祠留芳”列羊城八景之一。

20世纪20年代的陈家祠。这里曾办过广州最好的私塾——陈氏实业学堂，还曾设立过一所英文商业技术学校——广东公学，公学里所有的教师都在欧美受过高等教育。1917年，广州体育专科学校也建在这里。

The Chenjiaci Ancestral Hall in 1920's. The Chen's Enterprising School, a so called best private school in Guangzhou, used to be established here. Later, the Guangdong Public School, an English commercial school was set up here. The school teachers all had senior educational background in Europe and America.In 1917, the Guangzhou Junior College of Sports was founded here.

陈家祠的砖雕、灰塑、陶塑等，流畅剔透，精细入微。人物形态各异，再配上楼阁山景，就好像把连环画搬到了墙上。

In the Chenjiaci Ancestral Hall, all the brick carving, lime sculpture and clay sculpture are neat and delicate.The appearances of the figures are all different. With the background of buildings and hills, it's just like a story-book carved in the walls.

陈家祠神龛。陈姓在清代，是广东地区一大望族。旧时，陈家祠每年要举办春秋两次祭祀祖先的活动。20世纪50年代，这里举行过陈氏家族的最后一次祭祖活动。现在，林立的牌位早就撤了，只有做工精细的龛罩被保存了下来。

The shrine in the Chenjiaci Ancestral Hall.The Chen's family used to be a big clan in Guangdong Province in the Qing Dynasty. At that time, descendants of the Chen Clan worshipped their ancestors here twice a year in spring and autumn. The last worship activity was held here in 1950's, but now people can no longer see the spirit tablets here except for some delicate shrine utensil casings.

陈家祠的边门。

The wicket of the Chen-jiaci Ancestral Hall.

◎中山纪念堂　The Sun Yat-sen Memorial Hall

中山纪念堂位于越秀山南麓，今东风中路北侧。原址为清代抚标箭道，后为督练公所。北洋军阀统治时期为广东省督军署。1920年底至1922年孙中山在广州建立革命政权，这里曾是军政府和非常大总统府所在地。1922年6月，陈炯明兵变时，被夷为平地。为纪念孙中山，1928年3月在总统府旧址动工兴建纪念堂，1929年1月15日举行奠基典礼，1931年10月10日竣工。纪念堂由吕彦直设计，上海馥记营造厂承建。主体建筑占地面积3836平方米，总建筑面积6595.14平方米，是钢架和钢筋混凝土结构的宫殿式建设，为当时中国最大的会堂建筑。堂内空间疏阔，无一柱遮挡视线，成为中国近代建筑的代表作之一。1958年在堂前广场安放尹积昌等创作的孙中山雕像。中山纪念堂建成后一直是广州标志性建筑之一。

中山纪念堂奠基典礼场面。

The foundation stone laying ceremony of the Sun Yat-sen Memorial Hall.

1928年中山纪念堂施工工地。

The Sun Yat-sen Memorial Hall built in 1928.

中山纪念堂设计者吕彦直。曾就读清华学校、美国康乃尔大学，先后设计南京中山陵和广州中山纪念堂。1929年病逝，年仅35岁。

Lü Yanzhi is the designer of the Sun Yat-sen Memorial Hall, who studied in Tsinghua School and Comell University of USA. He is also the designer of the Sun Yat-sen Cemetery in Nanjing. Lü Yanzhi died in 1929, at the age of only 35.

20世纪30年代初的中山纪念堂。白色的花岗石基座和石阶、淡青色大理石裙墙，以及宝蓝色的石湾琉璃瓦顶，色彩鲜明和谐。

The Sun Yat-sen Memorial Hall in early 1930's. The granite foundation and staircases, the light green marble belt walls together with the Shiwan sapphire blue glazed tiles all look bright and harmonious.

作为 1945 年 9 月 16 日华南日军签降地点的中山纪念堂，见证了一段重要的历史。

The Sun Yat-sen Memorial Hall witnesses an important historic moment on September 16, 1945, when the Japanese invaders signed the Surrendering Agreement here.

◎黄花岗七十二烈士陵园 Mausoleum of the Seventy-two Martyrs at Huang-huagang

黄花岗七十二烈士陵园位于今先烈路。1911年“三·二九”广州起义失败后，革命党人潘达微冒着生命危险，收殓烈士遗骸72具，葬于黄花岗。1912年广东军政府决定拨款在黄花岗修建陵墓，但因政局动荡而未实施。1918年滇军师长方声涛（烈士方声洞之兄）募款修建，使之初具规模。其后续建墓亭、纪功坊、乐台、正门等建筑，至1935年建成全部陵园，占地面积13.6万平方米。主体建筑包括正门、陵墓和墓道。正门为巨型牌坊式门楼，上刻孙中山题词“浩气长存”。陵墓用花岗岩石块砌成基础，上立自由神雕像，中立云白色墓碑。墓后为纪功坊，用同盟会革命党海外各分支机构所献石块砌成。“黄花浩气”、“黄花皓月”为1986年、2002年评出的羊城八景之一。

20世纪20年代初陵园内的植树栏。

The tree planting railing in the Huang-huagang Cemetery in early 1920's.

潘达微像。同盟会员，起义失败后，他曾以《平民报》记者的身份在《平民报》上发表《咨议局前新鬼录，黄花岗上党人碑》一文，公开起义整个过程，同时宣布把红花岗改为黄花岗，取“残菊犹有傲霜枝”的诗意。当年入秋，潘在《平民画报》上又发表《黄花岗图》，并题句：“七十二坟秋草遍，更无人表汉将军。”

Pan Dawei, a member of the Tongmeng Party, wrote and published, as a news reporter of the Civil Daily, an article “Memorizing the Tongmeng Party members died in Huang-huagang” in the Civil Daily after the failure of the Huang-huagang Uprising, which made the whole uprisng process known to the public.At the same time, he had Hong-huagang renamed Huang-huagang because the dying chrysanthemum in the cold winter are believe to turn yellow.In the autumn of the same year, Pan Dawei wrote and published in the Civil Pictorial another article “The Picture of Huang-huagang” with the inscription——“Now the autumn grass has grown all over the grave, and people don't praise the General any more.”

20世纪30年代初陵园的墓亭和墓道。

The pavilion and tomb passage in the cemetery in early 1930’s.

◎十九路军坟场 Tombs of the soldiers of the Nineteenth Corps

十九路军坟场位于今先烈路沙河顶。1932 年为纪念国民革命军第十九路军在淞沪战役中阵亡的抗日将士，决定将正在建设中的国民革命军第十一军公墓改建为十九路军坟场。由著名建筑设计家杨锡宗设计并监造。1933 年后陆续建成，面积 5.2 万平方米。入口处有高约 16 米的花岗岩石砌成的仿罗马凯旋门式建筑，上端镌刻“十九路军淞沪抗日阵亡将士坟园”。背面门额上书“碧血丹心”。坟园主体建筑为巴罗克风格的半圆柱廊，柱廊前耸立一座高约 20 米的花岗岩石纪功柱，上立有一个肩托步枪的战士铜像，八个铜铸宝鼎排列在拱卫纪念碑的石栏基上。此外还有门亭、英烈题名碑、抗日亭、先烈纪念馆等建筑。抗战期间坟园遭受破坏。抗战胜利后，蒋光鼐、蔡廷锴等曾组织重修。1981 年辟为十九路军淞沪抗日阵亡将士陵园。

20 世纪 30 年代的坟场全景。

A full view of the cemetery in 1930's.

八只铜铸宝鼎在日军侵占广州期间被毁失去，20世纪90年代，广州市政府拨专款重铸复原。

The 8 precious copper pods were all destroyed when the Japanese invaded Guangzhou.The Guangzhou City Government had them rebuilt in 1990's.

象征性的水泥棺井然有序地排列着。实际上，阵亡将士的骸骨是集中掩埋的。

Concrete Coffins are arranged in order in the cemetery. In fact, the soldiers killed in the battle were buried all together in the cemetery.

象征胜利与光荣的凯旋门。十九路军多为广东人，故坟园建在广州。

The Arch of Triumph symbolizes victory and glory. The Cemetery is built in Guangzhou because most of the soldiers in the 19th Route Army are from Guangdong.

◎中央公园 The Central Park

中央公园建于 1921 年 10 月 12 日，位于清代抚署故址。因是广州第一座公立公园，故称第一公园。又因其位于市区中心，1925 年改名中央公园。园内布局呈几何对称状。民国时期，这里是广州花事活动之地，1930 年至 1949 年，曾先后举办过五次广州市菊花比赛会。1966 年，易名人民公园。20 世纪末，拆去围墙，成为一处绿化广场。

1921 年 10 月 12 日，在清代抚署故址建成的广州市第一公园，是广州最早建立的综合性公园。

The Guangzhou First Park was set up in the site of the Department in Qing Danasty in October 12，1921， which was the earliest comprehensive park in Guangzhou.

公园内的娱乐设施多种多样，图为公园内的音乐亭。

There are all kinds of amusement facilities in the Central Park. This is the Music Pavilion.

20世纪30年代的中央公园中心大道，其尽头是广州市府合署大楼。当日公园开放时，曾制定了《广州市第一公园游览规则》13条，体现了当时社会的文明程度。如第五条规定"园中木椅只可端坐，不得偃卧、竖足致失观瞻"。

In 1930's at one end of the Central Road inside the Central Park was the Guangzhou Government Comprehensive Building. On the day when the park was first opened to the public, the 13 Tourism Rules of the Guangzhou First Park were made, which reflected the social civilization of that period of time. The 5th Rule says "the wooden chairs in this park are only for seating, not for sleeping or stepping on."

公园内保存之大佛寺大钟。

The Big Clock of the Dafo Temple in the park.

◎越秀公园 The Yuexiu Park

越秀公园原称粤秀公园，位于今解放北路一带，由越秀山的自然景观开辟而成。越秀山自古就是揽胜之处，南越王赵佗曾在山上建越王台，故越秀山古名“越王山”。明永乐年间，山顶筑有观音阁，故又名“观音山”。1921年，孙中山在广州就任临时大总统时，下令将越秀山辟为粤秀公园。1925年12月，落成开放。1928年，在越秀山兴建广州植物园。1936年，改为中正林场。1945年易名越秀林场。1950年后重新建园。1957年广州市长朱光为公园题名越秀公园，同年11月7日开放。从元代“粤台秋月”、明代“粤秀松涛”、清代“镇海层楼”和“粤秀连峰”，到近年的“越秀远眺”、“越秀层楼”、“越秀新晖”，越秀山在新旧羊城八景中享有盛名。

20世纪30年代的粤秀公园。

The Yuexiu Park in 1930's.

20世纪30年代初越秀山公共体育场，已颇具规模。
The large Yuexiu Public Stadium in early 1930's.

20世纪50年代越秀公园的游人。
The tourists in the Yuexiu Park in 1950's.

◎ 海珠公园 The Haizhu Park

海珠公园位于今沿江西路新堤一横路附近，原址为珠江上的巨型岩礁，称海珠石，为历代羊城游览胜地。宋代建有慈度寺，其“珠江秋月”为宋羊城八景之一。明代修有文溪祠，其“珠海晴澜”为明羊城八景之一。清同治年间在此修筑海珠炮台。民国初年，成为军政机关办公地方。1925年10月由广州市工务局接收，定名海珠公园，并进行修整，1926年7月4日行开放典礼，遂成为市民悠闲胜地。1931年扩筑新堤，海珠石炸削沉埋地下，成为新堤的一段。海珠公园自此湮灭。

海珠公园全景。

The whole scene of the Haizhu Park.

海珠公园内景。

The interior of the Haizhu Park.

海珠公园内的程璧光像。1917年，程璧光率舰队南下广东，支持孙中山护法，任军政府海军总长。1918年2月在海珠公园原址遭暗杀。

The Statue of Cheng Biguang in Haizhu Park. In 1917, Cheng Biguang led his fleet to Guangdong in order to support Sun Yat-sen, and was appointed Navy Commander of the Military Government. Cheng was murdered right in the Haizhu Park in February, 1918.

◎永汉公园　The Yonghan Park

永汉公园位于今中山四路，原址属明清广东布政司署。清同治五年（1866 年），被法国强占为领事馆。1928 年，广州市政府收回建成动物园，取名永汉公园。1938 年冬广州沦陷后，该园成为华南日军的“靖国神社”。抗战胜利后，更名汉民公园。新中国成立后，先后改名人民公园、广州动物园。1958 年 6 月 1 日，改为儿童公园，占地面积 1.15 万平方米。

20 世纪 30 年代初的永汉公园大门。

The gate of the Yonghan Park in early 1930’s.

永汉公园里的动物棚。

The covered pen in the Yonghan Park.

20世纪40年代的汉民公园。

The Hanmin Park in 1940's.

◎文化公园 The Cultural Park

文化公园位于西堤二马路，原址是西堤居民住宅和商业区，抗战期间被炸成一片废墟，战后仍未能恢复。新中国成立后，在此废墟上筹建华南土特产展览交流会，1951年10月落成开幕。1952年改称岭南文物宫。1956年更名广州文化公园。党和国家领导人毛泽东、刘少奇、周恩来、董必武、陈毅等曾到公园参观。

1948年西堤灾区，满目疮痍。

The Xidi Disaster Area was severely afflicted in 1948.

1951年华南土特产展览交流会会场，面积11.76万平方米,共10个展馆。

The South China Local and Special Products Exhibition Fair in 1951. The fair had 10 exhibition halls, with the total area of 11760 m².

1955年的岭南文物宫，由中共中央华南分局第一书记、广东省政府主席、广州市市长叶剑英亲笔题写的宫名。

The Lingnan Cultural Relics Palace in 1955. The name of the palace was in the own handwriting of Ye Jianying, who was the first secretary of the South China Branch of the CPC, Governor of the Guangdong Provincial Government and Mayor of Guangzhou City.

20世纪60年代的文化公园，很长时间内是广州文化活动的“中心舞台”。

The Culture Park in 1960's. It served for quite a long period of time as the "Central Stage" of the cultural activities in Guangzhou.

3【经济掠影】

工商是广州的命脉。大工厂的创办和商业的繁荣，奠定了近代城市发展的基础。那些高大的厂房、轰鸣的机器，轩敞的商厦、琳琅的商品，成了广州人最富进取心的一张张名片。

◎石井兵工厂 The Shijing Arsenal

石井兵工厂即广东兵工总厂，因位于北郊石井而名。其前身为广州制造局，由两广总督张之洞创办，清光绪十三年（1887年）建成。初制枪弹，日产子弹8000发。光绪三十三年（1907年）扩充制造枪支和无烟弹。同年将制造局改为“广东制造军械局”，复改名“石井兵工厂”，继又改名“广东兵工总厂”。清宣统元年（1909年）增建一间生产火药的无烟药厂。1920年增设机器制造部门。20世纪30年代前期还先后增建手榴弹厂和发电厂。抗战前夕，该兵工厂迁广西贺县，继与广西兵工厂合并。抗战胜利后，工厂关闭。

1912年的石井兵工厂大门。

The gate of the Shijing Arsenal in 1912.

石井兵工厂生产的机关枪。

The machine gun made in the Shijing Arsenal.

石井兵工厂车间。

The Shijing Arsenal workshop.

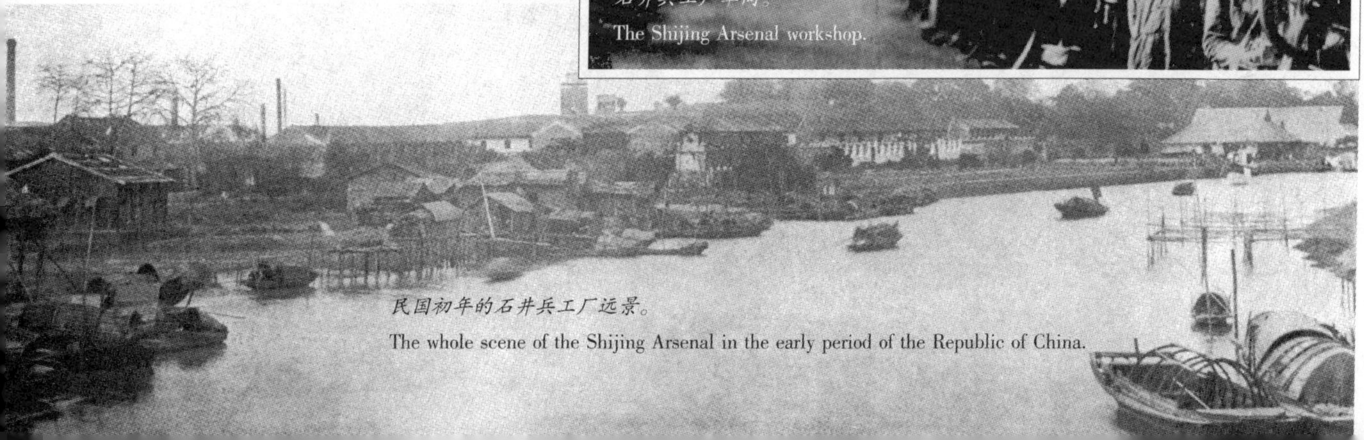

民国初年的石井兵工厂远景。

The whole scene of the Shijing Arsenal in the early period of the Republic of China.

◎广东士敏土厂 The Cement Plant of Guangdong

广东士敏土（即水泥）厂于清光绪三十二年（1906年）由两广总督岑春煊奏准开办，清宣统元年（1909年）建成投产，机器购自德国克虏伯格鲁森厂，厂址位于河南芳草围，初名“广东河南士敏土厂”。该厂是中国近代第二家士敏土生产企业，也是当时中国南方产量和规模最大的士敏土厂。1929年，为满足修建粤汉铁路所需的巨量士敏土，广东省建设厅在西村动工筹建广东西村士敏土厂，从丹麦史密斯公司购进日产200吨的先进湿制法机器。1932年6月建成投产。所产“五羊牌”水泥质量可媲美欧美各国产品。1933年7月1日，河南士敏土厂并入，成为广东西村士敏土厂河南分厂。1955年，西村士敏土厂改名为广州水泥厂。2003年4月，该厂迁移到花都。

河南士敏土厂全景和车间。士敏土厂的经营曾经历过商办、官商合办的模式，1932年才改为官办。

The full view and workshop of the Henan Cement Plant. It was once run by a private enterprise, then an official and private joint enterprise and at last by the government in 1932.

1932年建成的西村士敏土厂全景和车间。工厂建成时由国民党元老胡汉民题词，勒石为记。

The full view and workshop of the Xicun Cement Plant which was built in 1932. The Plant had the stone inscription of the senior KMT member Hu Hanmin when it was constructed.

◎协同和机器厂 Xietonghe Machine Factory

协同和机器厂创建于1912年，前身是清宣统三年（1911年）由陈沛霖、陈拔廷在芳村大涌口开办的协同和碾米厂。1912年与何谓文合股扩大成协同和机器厂，专门生产柴油机。1915年该厂成功仿制4缸44.3千瓦两冲程热球式柴油机。1918年又生产出117.7千瓦、用压缩空气启动、可逆转的两冲程柴油机，安装在轮船上航行于珠江，引起航运业重视，遂继续仿制了两冲程和四冲程柴油机多种。1930年在香港开设分厂。1937年，该厂累计生产了各种规格的柴油机383台/1.68万千瓦，有设备85台，职工340人，为华南地区最大的机器厂，产品行销华南、东南亚和加拿大等地。广州沦陷后，厂房设备遭日军劫掠一空。抗战胜利后，恢复机械维修业务。1956年，有9家小型机器厂并入，成为一家专业生产柴油机的工厂。1966年改名广州柴油机厂。

协同和机器厂的厂房和生产车间。

The factory building and workshop of the Xietonghe Machine Factory.

◎冯强胶鞋厂 Fengqiang Plastic Shoe Factory

冯强胶鞋厂是20世纪二三十年代广州最具实力的胶鞋厂，1921年由新加坡归侨肖侨鸿、司徒广和冯强等在泰康路设厂。主要产品是“大象牌”胶鞋。由于质量好，花色品种多，产品行销国内和东南亚一带。随着产品销路的拓展，工厂规模不断扩大，工人由原来的100多人增加到400多人，平均日产胶鞋由1000双增至5000～6000双，最高日产达9000双。1937年4月，由于日军入侵的影响，工厂被迫宣布解散。

20世纪二三十年代的冯强胶鞋厂的广告牌楼。

The advertisement archway of the Fengqiang Plastic Shoe Factory in 1920's and 1930's.

冯强胶鞋厂主人冯强。

Feng Qiang, the owner of the Fengqiang Plastic Shoe Factory.

20世纪30年代初冯强胶鞋厂粘鞋部。

The shoe sticking workshop of the Fengqiang Plastic Shoe Factory in early 1930's.

20世纪30年代初冯强胶鞋厂的车间。

The workshop of the Fengqiang Plastic Shoe Factory in early 1930's.

◎广东硫酸厂和广东苛性钠厂 Guangdong Sulphuric Acid Factory & Guangdong Caustic Soda Factory

1932年，广东省政府投资89万元，向美国化学建筑公司订购全套机器，在西村设厂，自制硫酸，1933年正式投产。该厂原称广东化学工业厂硫酸部，后改为广东硫酸厂。该厂是采用当时最新式的接触法生产硫酸的省营企业。1934年广东省政府又在西村工业区建成省营苛性钠厂，利用电解食盐的氯气和氢气合成法制造盐酸。1936年广东硫酸厂与广东省营苛性钠厂合并，改称广东硫酸苏打厂。抗战时期该厂先后六次遭日机轰炸，厂房设备被毁，无法复工。新中国成立后，广州市重新兴建了硫酸厂和生产盐酸的化工厂。

广东硫酸厂厂房。

The workshop of the Guangdong Sulphuric Acid Factory.

硫酸厂工人工作场景。

The workers working in the Sulphuric Acid Factory.

广东省营苛性钠厂厂房。

The workshop of the Guangdong Provincial Caustic Soda Factory.

苛性钠厂的固体苛性钠蒸镬。

The boiler of solid caustic soda in the factory.

苛性钠厂的盐酸吸收塔。

The hydrochloric acid absorption tower of the Caustic Soda Factory.

◎广东纺织厂 Guangdong Textile Factory

1933年广东省政府投资6340万元毫银，在广州河南芳草围兴建广东纺织厂，1935年建成投产，拥有棉、毛、丝织机共212台，设备大部分从英国进口，年产值220万元毫银，是广东第一间最具规模的现代化纺织企业。抗战期间，部分厂房被炸毁。抗战后复业，先后改名为广东实业有限公司广州纺织厂、广东实业有限公司纺织厂。新中国成立后，改名广东纺织厂。1968年改名为广州第一棉纺织厂。1990年该厂固定资产1.09亿元，年生产总值1.42亿元。

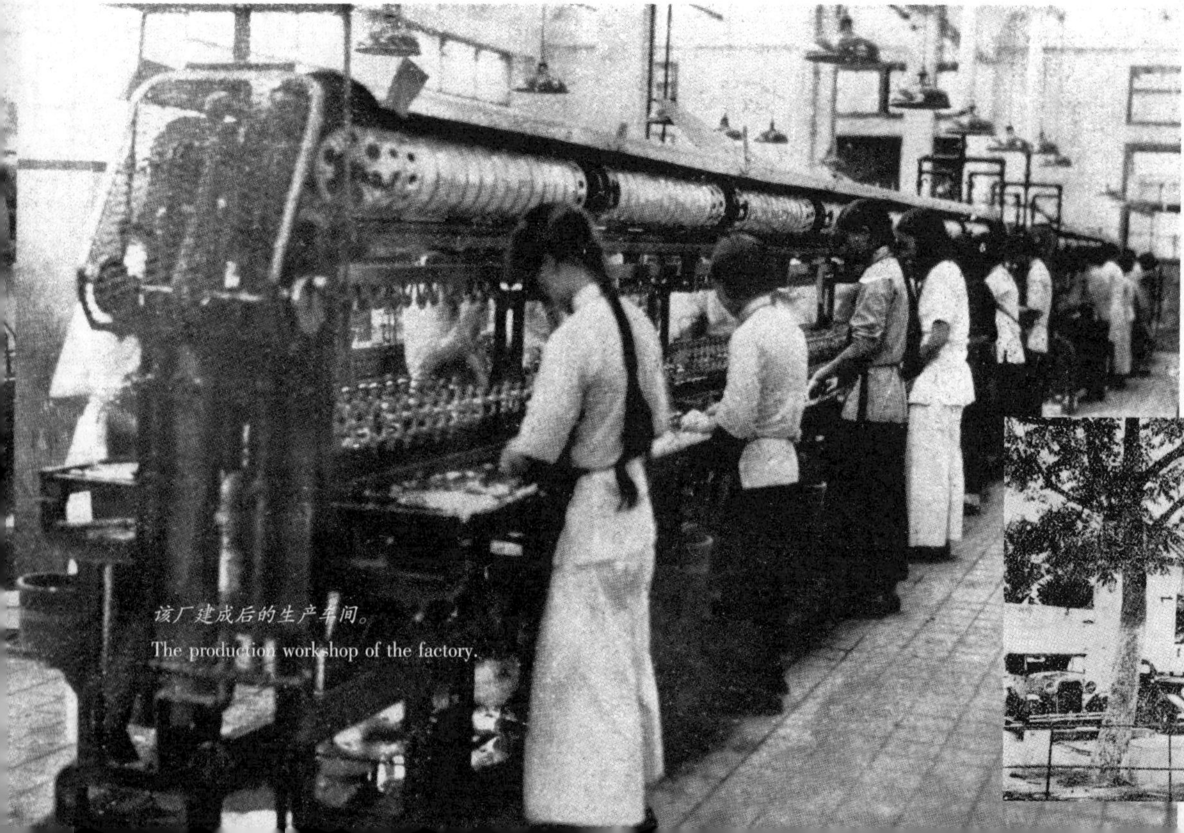

该厂建成后的生产车间。
The production workshop of the factory.

1936年广东纺织厂大门。
The gate of Guangdong Textile Factory in 1936.

生产车间。

Textile workshops.

◎增埗自来水厂 Zengbu Tap Water Works

增埗自来水厂建成于清光绪三十四年（1908年），生产能力为1350立方米/时，是广州第一间公用自来水厂。此前，广州居民饮用的是珠江河水或井水。该水厂初为官、商合办，1915年改为商办，1929年由市政府接管，并进行扩建，安装了第二套快滤式供水设备。新中国成立后，市政府进一步扩建增埗自来水厂。20世纪50年代末，其生产能力达到1.32万立方米/时，共有3套供水设备运转，后改称西村水厂。20世纪80年代以后，市政府又对西村水厂进行了改建、扩建，经过改造挖潜，1990年，西村水厂最大供水量达128万立方米/日，年供水量占全市年供水量的44.93%，成为全国三大自来水厂之一。

民国时期增埗自来水厂，以珠江、流溪河、小北江的混合支流为水源。

The Zengbu Tap Water Works in the period of the Republic of China.The factory draws the water from the joint stream of the Pearl River, the Liuxi River and the Xiaobeijiang River.

20世纪30年代该水厂的澄水池。

The filter pool of the factory in 1930's.

1907年建成的西关水塔，它是增埗自来水厂附设工程之一，1976年拆除。

The Xiguan Water Tower built in 1907. The tower, which was demolished in 1976, is one of the attached projects of the Zengbu Tap Water Works.

◎东山自来水厂 Dongshan Tap Water Works

东山自来水厂于1929年在广州杨箕村建成，日供水量270立方米，有效缓解了当时东山一带的缺水状况。1944年东山自来水厂被盟军飞机炸毁。新中国成立后，广州市公用局将百子路（今中山二路）泵房临时扩建为东山自来水厂。1953年市区向东输水干管调整，东山自来水厂遂停产。

20世纪30年代的东山自来水厂厂房。

The factory building of the Dongshan Tap Water Works in 1930's.

东山自来水厂水源——坡塘。

Potang——the source of water of the Dongshan Tap Water Works.

1934年夏广州市民在街边排队汲取公用自来水的情景。广州公用供水站直到20世纪70年代才从居民生活区消失。

In the summer of 1934, Guangzhou citizens queued for drink water in the street. All residential areas had had such public water supply centres until 1970's.

◎供电 Electric Power Supply

广州于清光绪十四年（1888年）开始使用电能，是国内最早使用电能的城市之一。光绪十六年（1890年），旅美华侨黄秉常等开办广州电灯公司，为国内民族资本最早经营的电灯公司。光绪二十七年（1901年），英商旗昌洋行在广州五仙门开办粤垣电灯公司，清宣统元年（1909年）被官商合组的广州电力股份有限公司赎回自办。1919年，广州电力股份有限公司转为民营，1932年被收归市营，由广州市电力管理委员会主管。1933年和1937年，广州河南电厂和西村电厂先后建成发电。日军侵华后，广州电力工业严重受毁。新中国成立后，广州市对发供电设备、线路等进行大修改造，使广州电网在全省电网建设中处于领先地位。1966年西村发电厂改名为广州发电厂。1978年黄埔发电厂建成，1990年装机容量增至110万千瓦，成为广东省最大的火力发电厂。

20世纪20年代初广州电力股份有限公司的电机厂。

The power factory of the Guangzhou Electric Power Stock Company Ltd in early 1920's.

20世纪30年代广州市电力管理委员会。

The Guangzhou Electric Power Administrative Committee in 1930's.

1933年2月15日广州河南电厂建成仪式上的场景。中立者为广州市市长刘纪文，戴眼镜者为广州市电力管理委员会委员陆匡文。

The inauguration ceremony of the Guangzhou Henan Electric Power Factory on Feb. 15, 1933. The man in the front middle was Liu Jiwen, Mayor of Guangzhou, and the man in glasses was Lu Kuangwen, member of the Guangzhou Electric Power Administrative Committee.

1933 年建成的广州河南电厂。

The Guangzhou Henan Electric Power Factory built in 1933.

◎黄埔港 The Huangpu Harbour

黄埔港是华南最大的沿海和远洋交通运输枢纽，位于广州市区东南的珠江口内。隋唐时期，黄埔港湾已是船舶进出广州的外港停泊地。孙中山先生生前即提议在黄埔建“南方大港”。1936年始建，次年建成400米沿岸码头，1939年投产。抗战爆发后，工程中断。40年代续建钢板桩码头，铁路专用线以及仓库、办公楼等辅助设施。新中国成立后，经过港区修复和航道疏浚，1950年10月复港。规模随后不断扩大，设施逐步配套。1973年开始开辟新港区。1987年末，码头岸线长5574米，万吨级码头泊位21个。黄埔港原属交通部黄埔港务管理局，1987年12月与广州港合并组成广州港务局。

20世纪30年代的广州黄埔码头。

The Guangzhou Huangpu Port in 1930's.

1948 年的黄埔码头。

The Huangpu Port in 1948.

◎邮政 Post

近代以前，广州民间书信传递的主要形式是民办专营通信的民信局。清末外国人开始在广州设立邮务机构，史称“客邮”。清同治五年（1866 年）广州海关始兼办邮政。清光绪二十三年（1897 年）大清邮政广州总局成立，清宣统三年（1911 年）改为广州邮政总局，次年更名为广东邮务管理局，邮政业务渐具规模。此后，客邮和民信局逐步停办。1936 年广州共有 21 间邮政支局，内设投递、分信、运输、快递、挂号、包裹等部门。从开办之日到广州沦陷，广州邮政管理局的重要职务多由英国人担任，一切规章全部效法英国。1938 年广州沦陷，粤北后方成立广东省邮政局驻曲江办事处，结束了洋人把持邮政的局面。

1916 年建成的广东邮务管理局大楼。由英国建筑师丹备勘图设计，为广州近代有代表性的欧洲新古典主义风格建筑。

The Guangdong Postal Service Administration Building built in 1916. The building, which was surveyed and designed by the British architect Denbigh, represents the typical European new classic architecture in modern Guangzhou.

民国初年设在岭南大学（今中山大学）的邮局。

The post office in Linnan University (now Sun Yat-sen University) in the early period of the Republic of China.

20世纪20年代初广州邮务管理局属下的乡间邮差，基本上是肩挑手扛，徒步送信。

The postman of the Guangzhou Postal Administrative Department in early 1920's. Carrying mails, they mostly sent letters on foot.

新中国成立初期广州市区的邮政投递员。

Postmen in the Guangzhou urban area in the early period when the People's Republic of China was just founded.

◎电信　Telecommunications

广州是中国电信业发展较早的城市。广州电信建设始于19世纪80年代，广州商绅集资筹建广州至香港陆上电报线。其后官督商办及官办的广州电报局和粤桂官电总局先后成立。清末和民国时期，广州电信门类陆续增加，在国内率先安装了无线电台。市内人工电话、自动电话、无线电长途电话等相继开通，为当时国内电信业务量较大的城市。1948年，广州电信局开通的电报直达电路共40路，长途电话电路共52路，广州市内自动电话有一个总所、两个分所，总机容量共9600门，但全市公用电话只有8部。

位于丰宁路（今人民中路）的广州市自动电话所，1928年建成。

The Guangzhou Auto-telephone Station was built in Fengning Road (now Renminzhong Road) in 1928.

1928年广州市普通电话接线员工作情景。

The phone switch board operators in Guangzhou in 1928.

20世纪30年代广州电话工人架设空中电缆的情形。

Guangzhou telephone workers were erecting phone cables in 1930's.

20世纪30年代广州电话工人安放地下通信电缆的情形。

Guangzhou telephone workers were laying underground cables in 1930's.

◎银行 Banks

清末，广州开始出现新式银行。最早是外商银行在广州设立的分支机构，其后，具有地方银行性质的官办广东官银钱局，中央政府官办的大清银行和交通银行广东分行，商办的大信银行等相继成立。民国成立后，由中国人自办的新式银行在广州迅速兴起，官办的有中央银行、中国银行广东分行、中国农民银行广州分行、广东省银行、广州市立银行等；民（私）营银行有广东银行广州分行、新华信托储蓄银行广州分行、东亚银行广州分行、金城银行广州分行等。这些银行按照西方银行原则进行组织和管理，业务不断拓展，在广州经济生活中发挥了重大作用。但由于政局不稳，这些银行时常处在动荡中。

清光绪十三年（1887年），两广总督张之洞在广州大东门外黄华塘街（今黄华路）筹建的广东钱局。1889年开炉试铸，为中国最早生产机制银元、铜钱的工厂。

In the 13th year of Emperor Guangxu of the Qing Dynasty (in 1887), Zhang Zhidong, governor of Guangdong Province and Guangxi Province, set up the Guangdong Bank in Huanghuatang street (now Huanghua Road), Dadongmenwai of Guangzhou. The coins, first made in 1889, were China's first machine made silver and copper coins.

20 世纪 30 年代成立的番禺县农民银行。

The Panyu County Peasants' Bank was set up in 1930's.

1924 年孙中山在广州南堤大马路（今沿江中路）创办的中央银行。

Sun Yat-sen set up the Central Bank in Nandi Road (now Yanjiangzhong Road) in Guangzhou in 1924.

20世纪40年代初期迁至粤北的广东省银行职员。

The Guangdong Provincial Bank clerks who moved to north Guangdong in early 1940's.

◎典当　Pawnshops

典当，亦称当铺或押店，是专门以收取抵押品而放款的古老的信用机构。由于旧时当押业利润可观，所以，民间有“若要富，开当铺”之说。19世纪下半叶开始，广州典当业迅速发展，出现当、按、押、小押几种典当铺，其门店规模、资本大小和期限长短各有不同。清末民初为广州典当业全盛时期，市区典当铺多达400多间。20世纪30年代以后，随着新的融资形式和融资渠道的大量出现，典当业逐步走向衰落。

图为民国初期广州的典当铺建筑。广州典当铺建筑呈方印形，状似高耸的炮楼，墙垣坚厚，窗户狭小，楼里储有石块、石灰用以防御火灾和强盗，还雇有保镖专人守护。

The Guangzhou Mortgage Building during the early period of the Republic of China looks like a square seal, and a tall blockhouse as well, with strong thick walls and small windows.Stone and lime were often stored in the building to prevent fire and robbers.And safeguards were employed to protect the building.

◎海关 Customs

清康熙二十四年（1685 年），清政府在广州五仙门设立粤海关，是当时中国四大海关之一。清乾隆二十三年至道光二十二年（1758 年至 1842 年）间粤海关为中国唯一的管理外商来华贸易的海关。第二次鸦片战争后，外国列强通过一系列不平等条约，攫取了中国海关管理权。清咸丰十年（1860 年）在西堤（今沿江西路）成立粤海关税务司署，管理权被外国人控制。美国人吉罗福充任税务司，英国人赫德、马察尔为副税务司，实行一整套半殖民化的海关制度。新中国成立后，粤海关改称“中华人民共和国广州海关”，直属国家海关总署，下设佛山、容奇、肇庆、韶关、白云机场等 10 个海关，在广州市内派驻 5 个办事处，负责监管进出境运输工具、货物、行李和邮递物品，征收关税和其他税费，查缉走私，编制海关统计等业务。

1916 年建成的粤海关大楼，俗称“大钟楼”。

The Guangdong Customs Building, colloquially called the Big Clock Building, was built in 1916.

清宣统二年（1910年）位于广州城西郊联兴街的粤海常关。

The Guangdong General Customs in Lianxinjie Avenue of Guangzhou west suburb in 1910 (the 2nd year of Emperor Xuantong of the Qing Dynasty).

清末粤海关黄埔分卡。

The Guangdong Customs Huangpu Branch in the late Qing Dynasty.

清宣统二年（1910年）建成的沙面粤海新关的公馆。

The residence of the Guangdong New Custom in Shamian was bulit in 1910 (the 2nd year of Emperor Xuantong of the Qing Dynasty).

位于五仙门的粤海常关（即原粤海关机构）办公楼，1931年改称为"粤海关民船管理处"。

The office building of the Guangdong General Customs (the former Guangdong Customs Department) at Wuxianmen of Guangzhou.It was renamed Management Department of Civil Boat of the Guangdong Customs in 1931.

◎街铺　Stores

清末民初，广州商业零售逐渐有了成行成市的特点，出现了各类专业街市。如下九路的金饰街、杨巷的布匹街、德星路的小百货街、长寿路的典当及医院诊所街、文昌路的家私街等，而批发店则多集中在同兴街、荣阳街、长寿里、吉星里等，零售以十八铺一带为最盛。并逐渐形成了相对集中和固定的服务对象：惠爱路（今中山路）、永汉路（今北京路）以军政界、教育界为对象，高第街做家庭妇女生意，河南以洪德路为繁盛，销售对象为居民和农民。清宣统元年（1909年）广州城区有店铺27524家，到1930年广州市区店铺达35946家，商业零售形成70多个自然行业。

1929年的广州水果铺。

A Guangzhou fruit shop in 1929.

20世纪40年代初期广州的海产批发市场。

A marine product wholesale market in Guangzhou in early 1940's.

20世纪40年代广州的水果批发市场。
A fruit wholesale market in Guangzhou in 1940's.

20世纪40年代广州的腊味铺。

A cured meat store in Guangzhou in 1940's.

◎日用品商店　Groceries

近代以前，广州日用品商店主要经营手工作坊和农村的手工业产品。鸦片战争后，洋货长驱直入，广州工匠在与洋货竞争中，对洋货逐步进行仿制和改造创新，形成了有地方特色的“广货”。清末广州经营日用工业品的行业约有 30 个。民国时期，广州日用品商店在经营品种、组织形式和管理方法等方面都起了很大变化，出现了由杂到专，由土转洋，华洋结合的更新。1929 年广州经营日用工业品的商店约有 767 家。当时大新公司经营的“环球百货”，实际上主要还是国货，兼营洋货。而洋货一般经由香港的总公司直接向外国厂商进货，以澳洲和美国货为主，后来多向日本购货。“九一八事变”以后，全国上下抵制日货，国货就成了公司经营的大宗。其时，大新公司还兼营亚洲酒店、觉天酒家以及理发、照相、餐饮等，整个“连锁”行业都以“百货”的招牌作号召了。

画家笔下清末广州的一家帽店，门面高敞，店内木制门窗雕刻精细考究。

A painting of a Guangzhou hat store which puts on a rather prosperous front. Inside, the door and windows are all delicately engraved.

20世纪40年代广州的绸缎商店。
A silk store in Guangzhou in 1940's.

1954年广州西堤百货商店（今南方大厦）。
The Xidi Department Store (now the Nanfang Mansion) in Guangzhou in 1954.

◎大新公司　The Daxin Company

20 世纪初，广州开始出现公司形式的百货店。1918 年，澳洲华侨蔡兴、蔡昌兄弟与其他侨商集资 40 万港元在广州西堤创办大新公司。它楼高 9 层，是 20 年代初期广州最高的大厦。地理位置也相当优越，临江的西堤一带历来就是商贸通衢，水陆四通八达，著名的十三行客流如云，公司在选址上占尽了地利。而它的建筑和设施更为时人所瞩目，它的 1 至 7 层是百货公司，8 至 9 层及天台建成游乐场所。不仅自置有供水、发电等设备，还装载了当时广州人罕见的 4 部升降机接载客人。在大厦的东侧还修筑了一条汽车道，方便小汽车盘

20 世纪 30 年代初的西堤大新公司。在爱群大酒店 1937 年建成前，曾是广州最高的楼宇。塔楼上原有以“大新”二字联缀的对子：“大好河山，四百兆众；新开世界，十二层楼。”

The Daxin Company Building in Xidi in early 1930's had been the tallest building in Guangzhou until 1937 when the Aiqun Hotel was built nearby. On the turret, there is a antithetical couplet which says: “ China has splendid mountains and rivers with 4 hundred million people; Guangzhou has this grand and splendid building as high as 12 storeys.”

大新公司创办人蔡兴。

Cai Xing, the founder of the Daxin Company.

旋而上顶层，出尽一时风头。引人注目的还有设在顶层的天台花园和天台游乐场，这里经常有所谓“文明戏”和杂耍等节目的演出，入场券每位一毫，一时游人如织，成为了宣传公司、吸引顾客的一种途径，又有“九重天”的雅称，是有钱有闲阶层游宴玩乐的去处。

但大新公司命途坎坷。1938 年广州沦陷前夕，曾被暴徒洗劫一空，沦陷时又遭焚毁，货物和设备均荡然无存。抗战胜利后，曾一度谋求复业，但资金筹措困难，一座华厦遂成废墟。直到 1952 年，政府拨款 150 万元人民币进行修复，重建为 12 层的南方大厦，于 1954 年国庆开业，再度成为广州最著名的百货大厦之一。

20 世纪 40 年代的大新公司。

The Daxin Company in 1940’s.

20 世纪 30 年代初惠爱路（今中山五路）大新分公司。又称“城内大新”，而西堤大新公司则叫“城外大新”。

The Branch Company of Daxin Company in Huiai Road (now Zhongshanwu Road) in early 1930's was called “ Inner City Daxin” while the company in Xidi was called “Outer City Daxin”.

◎先施公司 The Sincere Company

先施公司是民国时期广州规模最大的百货公司之一，1914 年由澳洲华侨马应彪在广州长堤创办。公司主营环球百货，兼营东亚大酒店、汽水厂、化妆品厂、玻璃厂、铁器厂、皮鞋厂、饼干厂，以及保险公司和信托银行。该公司在广州率先实行明码实价、窗橱陈列、分柜售货、多功能服务、专人开票收款、免费送货、固定营业时间、雇用女售货员等方式，深受顾客欢迎，并引领了当日的商业时尚。1935 年因资金周转不力，向香港汇丰银行借贷，实权落入汇丰银行手中。广州沦陷后，为汉奸李辅群占领，改为东亚百货公司。1946 年被接收回来，1948 年正式复业，但经营已大不如前。新中国成立后，市百货公司在首层和第二层开设中心百货门市部。1976 年原址毁于火。1984 年改建成 15 层的华厦公司。

20 世纪 20 年代的先施公司及其东亚大酒店。

The Sincere Company and its Oriental Hotel in 1920's.

先施公司创办人马应彪。

Ma Yingbiao, the founder of the Sincere Company.

20世纪20年代初先施公司的丝发部、香水部和德育部职员。

The clerks in the Shampoo Department, the Perfume Department and the Moral Education Department of the Sincere Company in early 1920's.

◎酒店　Hotels

酒店从旧时的客栈行发展而来。1914年澳洲华侨马应彪在长堤创办先施公司，并附设东亚大酒店，为广州最早的近代酒（旅）店之一。20世纪二三十年代是广州酒（旅）店业发展的高峰时期，集中在长堤、太平南路一带有新亚、爱群等一批中西合璧的酒店，成就了一派盛世浮华的景观。广州沦陷后，大批酒店撤往港澳，抗战胜利后，酒店业已经不复当日的光景了。

创建于1914年的长堤东亚大酒店。

The Oriental Hotel was built in Changdi in 1914.

建于1927年的太平南路新亚酒店。民国元老于右任手书店名。曾因管理上首倡“三不”（不得赌博、不得吸鸦片烟、不得宿娼）而卓有声誉。

The New Asia Hotel was built on Taipingnan Road in 1927. Yu Youren, the senior official of the Republic of China wrote the hotel name in his own hand.The hotel had been famous for its 3 NO's——No gambling, no smoking opium and no whoring.

20世纪30年代初长堤的中山大酒店。

The Zhongshan Grand Hotel in Changdi in early 1930's.

1937 年落成的爱群大厦。它是广州第一座钢框架结构的建筑，共 15 层，64 米高，外表宏伟，设备舒适，是沿江路最夺目的风景，曾在相当长一段时间里，为广州最高建筑。

The Aiqun Hotel built in 1937 is the first steel frame building in Guangzhou, which has 15 storeys and is 64 metres high with a grand outer look and lots of comfortable inner facilities. This buiding, which was then the most charming scene on Yanjiang Road, had been the tallest building in Guangzhou for quite a long period of time.

◎街招 Street Advertisement Signs

作为南方最大的商业城市，广州一向是商贾汇聚、街招林立。从前的街招形式多样，从竖招、横招、座招和墙招，到可摘挂和携带、常用于流动性经营的招幌等，一应俱全。清末广州小店铺一般只是挂幌子作标志，大商号则除挂字号牌匾外，门口还悬挂条匾，注明经营品种和业务特色。民国时期，随着广州商业街路面拓宽，街招的制作更趋讲究，样式更宏大。店号招牌也制作得更加精美，多为镶框木牌，以油漆书写。直至 20 世纪 50 年代初期，广州个别店号还保留古式招幌。20 世纪 80 年代以来，广州商家招牌多使用装潢精美的灯箱和徽标了。

清同治年间，广州幽远的长巷中招幌标立如旗。

There were all kinds of shop signs in the long lanes of Guangzhou during the period of Emperor Tongzhi of the Qing Dynasty.

20世纪40年代初期广州的街招。

The shop signs and advertisements in Guangzhou in early 1940's.

清末小市街的街招。

The shop signs in a small street in the late Qing Dynasty.

4 【教育概况】

教育是一个城市的灵魂。近代新式教育的拓展打开了广州人认识大千世界的窗口，建立起与外面世界更紧密的联系。在中西文明的交流中，一批批敢为天下先的学子一步步走向了世界。

◎广州贡院 Gongyuan in Guangzhou

清代广州贡院位于今文明路，是两广地区举行乡试的地方。始建于清康熙二十三年（1684年），当时有号舍5000间。清道光元年（1821年）号舍增至7603间。后毁于战火。清咸丰十一年（1861年）由两广总督劳重光重建。到清同治六年（1867年），整个贡院号舍已有11708间，规模宏大壮观，是清末中国四大贡院之一。广州贡院的号舍数十间为一列，形如长巷，每巷用《千字文》编列号数。号舍内置木板两板，分别作桌椅之用，休息时两木板合而为床。应试者入内即封号栅，食宿均在号舍内，俟交卷时方开。

清光绪三十一年（1905年）废科举后，广州贡院改建为两广速成师范馆等，也即后来广东大学和中山大学前期的校址所在地。

“学而优则仕”，贡院是封建时代无数士子平步青云的造梦场。士子们来此应试，如同向皇帝贡奉名产，因此叫贡院。从照片上宽阔的甬道和两侧排布谨严的号舍，足可想见当年肃穆紧张的气氛。

As a Chinese saying says, “He who once passes the exam becomes a government official”, Gongyuan (Institute of Tribute) is an important place where thousands of examinees made every effort to realize their dreams in the old feudal period of China. Examinees regarded their taking the tests as tributing well-known products to the Emperor, thus it’s called the Institut the of Tribute. The wide main road with the neatly designed dorms on both sides reflects the solemn and tense atmosphere there.

清末广州贡院的号舍。乡试每三年举行一次，考期在八月，分三场，考中的称为举人。应试入场前要经过唱名、搜检等极其严格的手续，答卷时外有兵丁监视，形同罪囚，而稍有不慎，往往即被拖出场去，时人多有“斯文扫地”之诮。那时考试不限年龄，可以活到老，考到老。号舍内坐着白发萧萧的老贡生，也是常有的事。

The dorms of Gongyuan in the late Qing Dynasty. The local exam was usually held in August every 3 years with 3 sections.He who passes will be honorably entitled “Juren”. Examinees should report their names and be body searched before taking the exams. Soldiers outside keep inspecting the examinees while they are answering the test papers, which is like inspecting criminals.If someone cheats, he will be thrown out immediately. People often saw elderly grey-haired examinees taking part in the exam because there was no age limit for candidates at that time.

◎岭南大学 Lingnan University

岭南大学前身是美国传教士于清光绪十四年（1888 年）创办的格致书院，光绪二十六年（1900 年）迁澳门，改名岭南学堂。光绪三十年（1904 年）迁至广州河南康乐村，不久开办大学预科，1912 年更名岭南学校，1914 年改为岭南文理科大学。1927 年岭南大学由国人收归自办，钟荣光为首届华人校长，孙科任董事会主席，为拥有文、理、工、农、医、商、神学院以及附属医院的华南最完备的私立大学。岭南大学外籍教师较多，最多时达四五十人。新中国成立后，与中山大学合并，部分系科调整到其他院校。

20 世纪 30 年代初岭南大学校园花木繁盛。当年钟荣光提倡在校园里广植有经济价值的果木，树人树木，遗泽广披。

There was a lush growth of trees and grass on the campus of Lingnan University in early 1930's. Principal Zhong Rongguang suggested that more economic plants should be planted on the campus so as to cultivate students and fruit trees at the same time.

20世纪30年代初的岭南大学码头。

The Lingnan University Port in early 1930's.

1918年的岭南大学第一届毕业生李汝俭、陈廷恺和卢家炳。

Li Rujian, Chen Tingkai and Lu Jiabing are the first graduates of Lingnan University in 1918.

1931年岭南大学校长钟荣光与长期主持岭南大学纽约董事局事务的格兰氏合影。钟荣光是岭南大学的第一位华人校长，也是中国教会大学华人校长第一人，被尊称为“红灰慈父”（红灰是岭南大学的校色标志）。他于1937年曾自撰挽联：“三十年科举沉迷，自从知罪悔改以来，革过命，无党勋；作过官，无政绩；留过学，无文凭；才力总后人，唯一事工，尽瘁岭南至死。两半球舟车习惯，但以任务完成为乐，不私财，有日用；不养子，有徒众；不求名，有记述；灵魂乃真我，几多磨练，荣归基督永生。”

Principal Zhong Rongguang of Lingnan University and Mr.Grant, who had been, for quite a long time, in charge of the New York Board of Directors affairs of Lingnan University in 1931. Zhong Rongguang, who was then respectfully called “Father of Red Gray” (red gray was the distinguishing mark of Lingnan University), was the first Chinese principal of Lingnan University, and the first Chinese principal of missionary universities in China. In 1937, Zhong Rongguang wrote a elegiac couplet to describe himself——“It has been 30 years since I took the imperial examinations.After growing up to be sensible and intelligent enough, I took part in the revolution but without any merit; I once secured an official position but without any achievement; I studied abroad getting no diplomas. Realizing that I am not as smart as others, I keep doing things in a diligent and serious way so as to work hard for Lingnan University. Getting used to living in China and abroad, I take great pleasure in working unselfishly. Having no children but a large number of students, I seek no personal fame. Having been in persuit of a pure heart, I owe everything of myself to Jesus Christ.”

1919年岭南大学的化学试验室。岭南大学教学水平接近发达国家同类大学，其毕业生只需再补修30个学分，就可进入美国的研究生院。而农学院的毕业生由校长介绍，可不需考试直入美国哥伦比亚大学、耶鲁大学等校就读。

The chemistry lab of Lingnan University in 1919. The teaching level of Lingnan University was almost the same as universities of the same kind in developed countries.The graduates only needed to get 30 more supplementary credit points to go to American post-graduate institutes. And the graduates of the College of Agriculture, recommended by the principal, could directly go to study in Columbia University or Yale University in USA without taking any examinations.

◎中山大学　Sun Yat-sen University

中山大学前身是1924年创办的国立广东大学，由原广东高等师范学校、广东农业专门学校和广东法政大学合并而成。1926年为纪念孙中山先生，改校名为国立中山大学。1935年迁校至广州东郊石牌。中山大学先后共设文、法、理、工、农、医、师范七个学院，是多学科的综合性大学。邹鲁、戴传贤、朱家骅、许崇清、金曾澄等人先后任校长。新中国成立后，以中山大学和岭南大学两校文理学院为基础合组新的中山大学。

为纪念孙中山先生，1926年7月17日，国民政府发布命令，正式宣布广东大学改名为中山大学。图为该校正门。

In order to commemorate Dr. Sun Yat-sen, the government issued a decree and officially announced that the Guangdong University was changed its name to Sun Yat-sen University in July 17, 1926. The picture shows the main entrance of the school.

位于文明路原广州贡院的中山大学校门。时为20世纪30年代初，墙壁上的校训“明耻、立信”等字格外醒目。该校藏书甚丰，1931年已达24.26万册，在全国公私立大学中排行第二。

The gate of the Sun Yat-sen University in the former Gongyuan on Wenming Road in early 1930's. The school motto on the wall says "Learning to the tell the good from the bad, and be unswervingly true to promise". The large collection of books in the university, which was as many as 242,600 copies in 1931, ranked the second in all the state-run and private universities and colleges in the whole country.

1935年迁校至广州东郊石牌后的中山大学校门。

The gate of the Sun Yat-sen University which moved to Shipai of Guangzhou east suburb in 1935.

1936年的中山大学文学院。当时中山大学规定，学生凡每种必修课目分数均在75分以上，各课程总平均分在85分以上者，酌予免缴学费或奖适用书籍；凡品行端正、学业优良之贫苦学生，酌予贷金。

Institute of Literature in Sun Yat-sen University in 1936. According to the university regulations, students whose required course grades are all 75 or above, and the average of all courses is 85 or above, will be remitted from tuition fees, or get a reward of textbooks.Students who are from poor families and of good character and fine scholarship will be granted a loan.

1929年中山大学语言历史学研究所的部分研究人员。中山大学在成立的最初几年里，采取聘请外国专家、教授来校任教，以及将年轻优秀的助教送出国深造，作为提高教学质量和学术水平的有力措施之一。

Some researchers of the Institute of Languages and History of Sun Yat-sen University in 1929. During the early years when the university was newly founded, foreign experts and professors were employed to teach here, and meanwhile, young teachers were sent abroad to have further study, which served as one of the important measures to improve the teaching quality and academic level of the university.

◎广东国民大学 Guangdong National University

私立广东国民大学创办于 1925 年，1928 年设立文学院、法学院和商学院。校址初设在东山，后在多宝路荔湾桥西建筑新校舍。又在惠福西路增设分教处。1930 年增设工学院。陈其瑗、吴鼎新等先后任校长。新中国成立后，并入华南联合大学。

惠福西路的校舍。当时广东国民大学各系分设日班、夜班，春季、秋季几种学制。解决了大批青年求学问题，颇受社会欢迎。

The college on Huifuxi Road. All departments of Guangdong National University had day classes, night classes, spring classes and autumn classes, which were at that time quite popular, so as to solve the problem of young people of all levels who were eager to study in the university.

20世纪30年代中期的校舍。

The university in mid 1930's.

20世纪30年代初部分学生的合影。广东国民大学得力于海外侨胞的赞助颇大。校务的经常开支，校舍的兴建，设备的购置，多有赖于华侨的捐助。

Some of the university students in early 1930's. Guangdong National University was under the auspices of oversea Chinese who largely supported the university in its daily expenses, building constructing and facility purchase.

1930 年该校学生业余时间打网球的场面。

Students of the university playing tennis in spare time in 1930.

◎孙逸仙博士医学院　Dr.Sun Yat-sen Medical College

孙逸仙博士医学院的前身是博济医院附设的博济医学堂，清同治四年（1865年）由美国医学博士嘉约翰创办，是中国最早的西医专科学校，孙中山先生早年曾在此学习。清光绪二十九年（1903年）正式称南华医学堂，附属于博济医院。1930年博济医院移交岭南大学。1936年，岭南大学以博济医院为基础，创办孙逸仙博士医学院，作为岭南大学医学院，原博济医院则作为医学院的附属医院。新中国成立后，孙逸仙博士医学院并入中山医科大学，附属医院成为中山医科大学附属第二医院，1985年称孙逸仙纪念医院。

1937年该学院一景。院内矗立着纪念碑，上书“孙逸仙博士开始学医及革命运动策源地”。

The Sun Yat-sen Institute of Medical Sciences.Visitors can see “The place where Doctor Sun Yat-sen learnt medicine and began the revolution movement” on the monument in the institute.

1938 年该学院几位教务人员合影。

Some of the staff of the institute in 1938.

20 世纪 30 年代后期该学院附属医院的一间病房。

One ward of the hospital attached to the institute in the late 1930's.

20 世纪 30 年代该校教职员合影。

The stuff of the medical college in 1930's.

该校男生第一宿舍。

The first male student dormitory of the college.

◎光华医学院 Guanghua Medical college

位于五仙门前的私立光华医学院于清光绪三十四年（1908 年）三月，由广州一批西医创办。开创了由中国人自办、中国人任教、用中文讲课的西医教育新纪元。初名光华医学堂，取名光华，意在“光我华夏”。其后改名为私立广东光华医科专门学校和私立广

东光华医科大学。1929年正式称私立光华医学院。学制初为4年，后改为5年。1929年经教育部核准正式立案后，学制延长为6年。著名学者陈垣为该校早期毕业生。新中国成立后，该校并入华南医学院，即后来的中山医科大学。

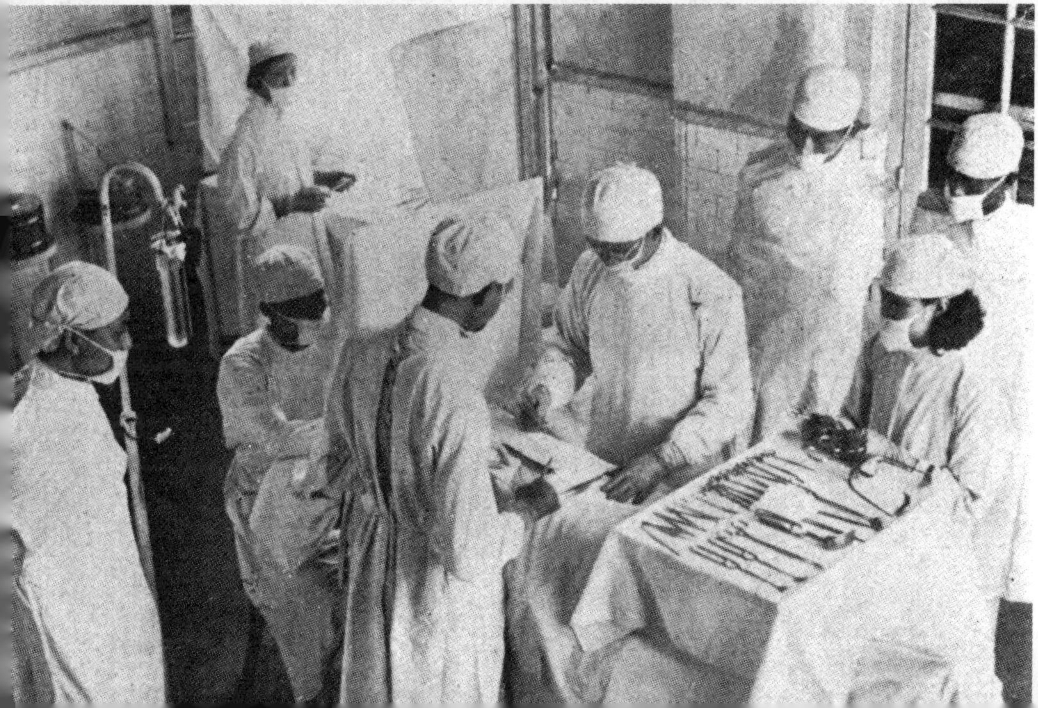

20世纪30年代该校病理学实验室和附属医院的外科手术室。

The pathology lab of the college and the surgical operation room of the attached hospital in 1930's.

◎广州女子师范学校 Girl's Normal School of Guangzhou

省立广州女子师范学校创办于清光绪三十三年(1907年)，初名官立女子初级师范学堂，以大石街太清宫旧址为校舍。该校招生入学条件：清白、健康、端敏，年龄17～18岁。考入后要经过3个月的“甄别”。其文史科教师均聘自省内女名流，另聘日籍女教师担任图、工、乐、体课程。由于女数学教师难找，只好破例聘年龄50岁以上的一名男教师。民国成立后，改称广东省立女子师范学校，1923年扩充莲塘路（今吉祥路）旅粤中学故址为师范部，大石街校址改为小学部。1928年该校又改为广东省立第一女子师范学校。1935年更名为广东省立广州女子师范学校。抗战期间曾先后迁校于南海西樵和粤北的曲江、连县等地。新中国成立后，一度仍为广东省立女子师范学校，后停办。

20世纪20年代末该校大门一侧。

One side of the school gate in the end of 1920's.

民国时期该校教学楼。

The teaching building of the school during the period of the Republic of China.

抗战前期迁至南海西樵简村的临时校舍。

The temporary school building at Jiancun Village, Xiqiao of Nanhai County during the early period of the Anti-Japanese War.

抗战前期该校学生在简村一间小学校中实习授课的场面。试教是广州女师实习程序的一项，记分标准是：教案30%，教学技能50%，观摩20%。

The normal school student having teaching practice in a primary school in Jiancun Village during the early period of the Anti-Japanese War. Trial teaching was one of the teaching practice procedures for a Guangzhou Female Normal School student, the grading standard of which usually included teaching plan (30%), teaching skill (50%) and observing & emulating (20%).

◎广州市立美术专科学校 The Municipal Academy of Art

广州市立美术专科学校创办于1922年，是全国建校最早的公立美术学校。1923年先后设立西洋画科、中国画科、艺术师范科和图案画科，教育局长许崇清，著名画家胡根天、李金发等先后任校长。画家赖少其、李桦、吴琬、刘仑、唐英伟等都是该校毕业生。该校1938年停办。

20世纪30年代初该校大门，位于惠爱西路（今中山六路惠爱市场）。创办初期校址在中央公园东北角，后一度迁至越秀山麓三元宫旁。

The school gate on Huiaixi Road (now the Huiai Market on Zhongshanliu Road) in early 1930's. The school was at the northeast corner of the Central Park when it was newly founded, and later moved to the Yuexiu Hill foot, near Sanyuangong Palace.

该校国画课室。每个学生画案上都摆放一瓶插花。

A vase of flowers was put on each student's desk in the Chinese painting classroom of the school.

该校西洋画课室的人体写生。该校注重基本功训练，专业课之外还设外语、美学、人体解剖、艺术史、色彩学等有关课程。

Portrait from human bodies of the western painting class of the school. Basic skill training is specially stressed in this school. Besides specialized courses, students also learn foreign languages, aesthetics, human body anatomy, art history and chromatography.

◎广州市职业学校 Guangzhou Municipal Vocational School

20 世纪 20 年代初至 30 年代初，广州市先后兴办了三所市立职业学校。市立第一职业学校创办于 1922 年，是广州最早的公立职业学校，初名市立女子缝刺学习所，后改为广州市立女子职业学校，1932 年更名市立第一职业学校，主要专业有缝纫、刺绣、图书管理和公务等，新中国成立后停办。市立第二职业学校创办于 1928 年，主要专业有土木工程、汽车驾驶修理、机械工程、电气工程等，广州沦陷后停办。市立第三职业学校创办于 1933 年，专业有应用化学、印刷制版和电气工程，1936 年停办。

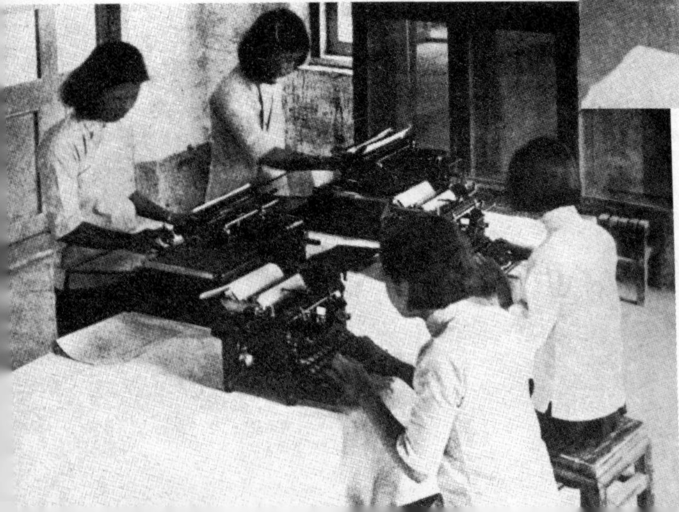

市立第一职业学校的学生在练习刺绣和打字。该校设在西湖路，以女学生为主。

Students of the Guangzhou City First Vocational School are practising embroidering and typewriting.The school is on Xihu Road, and the students are mainly girl students.

市立第二职业学校的学生在实习机械操作。该校原址在西关高岗，后迁至东沙路淋水岗，该校办学十余年，共培养学生近600名。

Students of the Guangzhou Municipal Second Vocational School are practising operating machinery. The school, which was originally at Gaogang of Xiguan but later moved to Linshuigang of Dongsha Road, kept running for 10-odd years, and nearly 600 students graduated from the school.

市立第三职业学校的学生在实习排字。该校设在河南凤凰岗，在设科上与市立一、二职有所分工，为高级职业学校。

The students of the Guangzhou Municipal Third Vocational School are practising typesetting. The school, which is at Fenghuanggang, Henan, is quite different in course design from the 1st and the 2nd vocational schools because it is regarded as a senior vocational school.

◎真光中学 Zhenguang Middle School

真光中学前身是美国基督教长老会的那夏理女士于清同治十一年（1872年）创办的真光书院，它是广州最早的教会学校，也是广州最早的女子学校。1917年改校名为私立真光女子中学，成为广州设置最早的一所女子中学。首任校长是美国人祁约翰博士。1930年美国教会将学校移交华人办理。新中国成立后，一度改为广州市第二十二中学等，1984年复名真光中学。

该校创办人那夏理女士。

The school founder Ms. Nal Shelly.

该校初创时的校舍，位于沙基（今六二三路）。

The school was at Shaji (now Liuer-san Road) when it was first founded.

真光中学初创时招收的学生，当时只招了30名女学生，多是已婚女子。

Student of the Zhenguang Middle School which was then newly founded. The school only recruited 30 students who were mainly married women at that time.

清光绪二十八年（1902年）该校学生集会的场面。该校校训是“崇实求真”，提倡“严、勤、实、勇、礼、静、洁、美”的校风。

Students of the school are having a meeting in 1902 (the 28th year of Emperor Guangxu of the Qing Dynasty). The school motto is “Seeking honesty and truth”, and the school spirit is “Being strict, hard-working, honest, brave, polite, calm, tidy and nice-looking”.

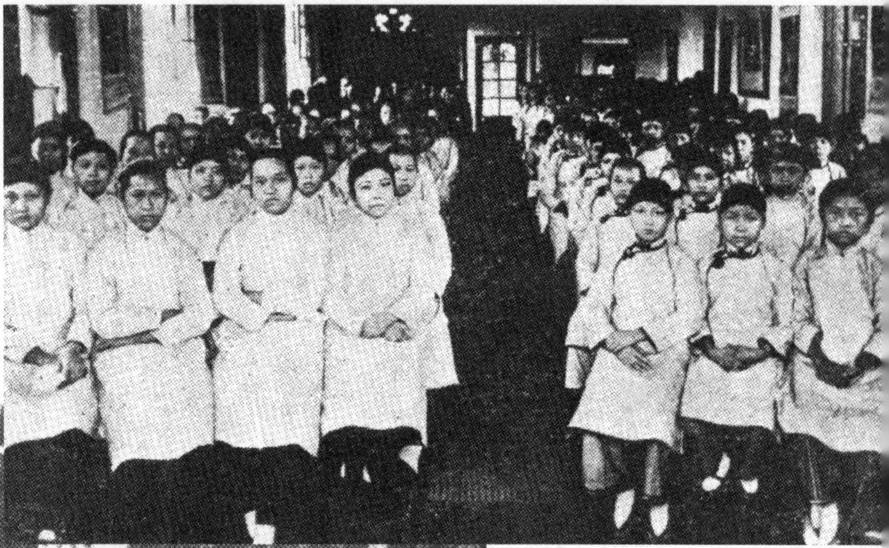

清宣统元年（1909年）该校师范班学生的合影。真光女中以管理严格著称，培养了不少人才，校友遍布海内外。

Students of the normal class of the school in 1909. (the 1st year of Emperor Xuantong of the Qing Dynasty). The school, which is well-known for her strict management, nurtured and educated quite a large number of talented students who were both at home and abroad.

◎广雅中学　Guangya Milddle School

位于西村的广雅中学前身为清末两广总督张之洞于清光绪十四年（1888年）创办的广雅书院，以“广者大也”、“雅者正也”而命名。后曾更名两广大学堂和广东高等学堂等，1912年称广东省立第一中学，1922年，该校实行初高中各三年的新学制，为广东旧制学校试验新学制之始。1928年改名广东省实验中学，1935年更名为广东省立广雅中学。著名学者黄节、梁漱溟等先后任校长。新中国成立后，曾一度更名为广州市第五十四中学，1978年复名广雅中学。

20世纪30年代该校图书馆——冠冕楼。广雅中学在教学上一向提倡启发式教学法，鼓励学术讨论，推广课外阅读。

The school library——the Guanmian Building in 1930's. The Guangya Middle School had been promoting elicitation method of teaching and encouraging academic discussion and students' outside reading.

九曲桥畔观风荷，这是广雅校园内的九曲桥。

Looking at the pretty lotus on the Jiuqu Bridge on Guangya school campus.

广雅中学提倡“教、学、做”合一精神，重视实验与讲课相结合。课外活动内容非常丰富。这是20世纪30年代该校学生生活的几个场面。

The Guangya Middle School promotes the combination of “teaching, learning and practising” by encouraging both doing experiments and giving lectures. Thus, students have a lot of outside classroom activities.The photos here show the students’ school life in 1930’s.

娱乐。

Recreational activity.

劳动。

Students working in the field.

◎培道中学 Peidao Middle School

培道中学前身是清光绪十四年（1888 年）由美国浸信会创办的培道女学，校址原在广州五仙门，光绪三十四年（1908 年）迁现址东山寺贝通津，1919 年更名私立培道女子中学。1923 年实行新学制，设初、高中及附属小学，并附设华侨班。其后，学校逐渐改由华人自办。新中国成立后，曾改名为广州市第二女子中学等，现为广州市第七中学。

民国时期该校的宗教院。

The Institute of Religion in the school during the period of the Republic of China.

20世纪30年代该校部分师生合影。

Some of the teachers and students of the school in 1930's.

1933年该校的生物实验室。

The school biological lab in 1933.

◎南武中学 Nanwu Middle School

南武中学前身是清光绪三十一年（1905年）由南武公学会在海幢寺园照堂创办的南武两等小学堂。“南武”取义于广州城曾名南武城。初办时只有学生16人。1912年，更名南武中学，是当时最有名的私立学校之一。1924年迁到同福中路。该校重视体育教育，为国家培养出不少体育人才。曾与天津南开中学齐名，有“南北两南”之称。谢英伯、何剑吴等人先后任校长。新中国成立后，南武中学先后更名广州第十九中学、广州市实验学校和广州市第五十八中学。1984年复名南武中学。

20世纪20年代初该校全体教职员的合影及校务处办公场面。

The school staff and the School Affairs Office in early 1920's.

上图为20世纪20年代初该校学生自治会成员合影。

下图为该校童子军操练旗语的情景。

Members of the Students' Self-management Union of the school in early 1920's.

The school boy scouts drilling semaphore.

◎执信中学 Zhixin Middle School

执信中学初名私立执信学校，创办于1921年，是为纪念朱执信先生而由孙中山先生提议创办的。校址原在清泉路（今应元路）应元书院，1925年迁到东沙路竹丝岗（今执信南路）。1928年更校名为省立执信女子中学。曾醒、金曾澄等先后任校长。新中国成立后，一度改名为广州市第五十五中学，1978年复名执信中学。

20世纪30年代初校园一景。
The school campus in early 1930's.

建校初期曾是男女同校，1928 年，广东省教育厅下令男女分校，于是改为女中。该校抗战期间迁往粤北，改为“省立执信中学”，同时招收男女学生。抗战胜利后，回到广州，又恢复为女校。

There were both boy students and girl students in the school when it was then newly founded.In 1928, it became a girls' middle school according to the order that boys and girls should be separated in different schools by the Guangdong Education Department. The school moved to north Guangdong during the Anti-Japanese War and was renamed "Provincial Secondary School of Zhixin", enrolling both boys and girls.And after the victory of the War, it was restored to a girls' school when moving back to Guangzhou.

1927年该校女生救护队进行模拟训练的场面。

The girl ambulance corps are having simulated training in 1927.

◎广州市第一中学　Guangzhou NO.1 Middle School

广州市立第一中学创办于1928年，是广州最早的市立学校。原址在一德路石室附近，1929年迁校址于越秀山麓，这里曾是广州著名的书院——学海堂和应元书院的所在地。该校抗战期间停办，1945年9月复办，地址改在蓬莱路原市立二中校址。新中国成立后仍为广州市第一中学。

20世纪30年代初，位于越秀山麓的校园全景及学校教务和事务人员办公场面。

A whole view of the school from the Yuexiu Hill foot in early 1930's. School staff working in the office.

20世纪30年代初，学校图书馆阅览室

The school library reading-room in early 1930's.

◎盲人教育 Education of the Blind

广州市的盲人教育始于清末。两广总督张之洞在任期间曾在广州创办瞽目院。从清光绪十七年（1891年）开始，美国教会在广州先后开办了明心瞽目学校和慕光瞽目院。1924年广州市政府曾将清末瞽目院一部分划出开办盲人学校。1926年广州市政府创办了市立贫民教养院，接管瞽目院，1931年又将包括盲人在内的残废院改为健济院。1933年广州市贫民教养院改为广州市救济院，其中的健济院改为教养所，广州沦陷后停办。这些图片为1933年初在广州市第一次展览会上，健济院的盲人们进行技能学习表演的场景。

授课。

Having a class.

下棋。

Playing chess.

编织。

Knitting.

演奏。

Playing musical instrument.

打字。

Typewriting.

◎女学生　Girl Students

广州女性正式接受近代学校教育，始于19世纪70年代的教会学校，至20世纪初期，广州教会女子教育已进入高等教育阶段。清光绪三十三年(1907年)，清政府颁布《女子小学堂章程》，正式规定女子有受教育的合法权。此后，广州开始有了普通女子师范教育和小学教育。民国成立后，有了普通女子中学。从1917年起，广州高等院校逐步实行了男女同校。但社会上仍然普遍重男轻女，如1928年，广州市教育局规定，广州市立小学毕业生，每班挑选一名成绩最优的男生免试升学，倘该班毕业生第一名属女生，则以第二名男生选送，以此类推，如该班至第5名均无男生，则该班不予选取。女学生之受轻视可见一斑。

清末夏葛女医学堂的女学生。

Girl students of the Xiage Female Medical School in the late Qing Dynasty.

清末真光书院的女学生。

Girl students of Zhenguang School in the late Qing Dynasty.

1919 年岭南学校的女生。

Girl students of Lingnan School in 1919.

1935 年广东省立广州女子师范学校的女生。

Girl students of Guangzhou Girl's Normal School of Guangdong Province in 1935.

◎学生管乐队　Student's Wind Band

西洋乐器是通过西方传教士进入广州的。清末，随着废除科举、兴办学校，广州部分学校开始出现管乐队。民国成立后，很多学校，尤其是教会学校和华侨办的学校都纷纷成立起学生管乐队。

民国初年广东高等师范学校的管乐队。

The wind band of Guangdong Senior Normal School during the early period of the Republic of China.

20世纪30年代岭南大学附中的学生管乐队。

The students' wind band of the Middle School Attached to Lingnan University in 1930's.

20世纪30年代广州执信中学学生管乐队训练的场面。

The students' wind band of Guangzhou Zhixin Middle School practising playing in 1930's.

20世纪40年代初广州童子军管乐队在街头表演的场面。

The Guangzhou Boy Scouts Wind Band performing in the street in early 1940's.

◎童子军　Boy Scouts

童子军是民国时期的一种少年军事训练组织。1915 年，广州开始出现童子军组织，1917 年，中华童子军广东支部和童子军研究会相继在广州成立，随后广州市中学和高小纷纷组织起童子军。1927 年 4 月，中国国民党童子军广州市军部成立。从 1929 年起，广州市全面在中学初中以及中等技术学校中设置童子军课程，推行童子军管理。1932 年在初中生中正式建立童子军团。童子军训练内容主要有纪律、礼节、操法、结绳、旗语、侦察、救护、炊事、露营等，学生的童军课成绩并入体育成绩中。

1927 年 4 月 12 日在中山大学举行的童子军广州市军部成立典礼上，童子军领袖班成员的合影。

Members of the boy scouts leader class in the inaugural ceremony of the Boy Scouts Guangzhou Military Department held in Zhongshan University on April 12, 1927.

1933 年参加“三八”节活动的女童军。

Girl Scouts taking part in the Women's Day activities in 1933.

1934 年广州女童军的露营训练。

Guangzhou Girl Scouts having camp drills in 1934.

1935年在第十三次广东省运动大会上广州童子军的滑布表演。

Guangzhou Boy Scouts performing cloth sliding in the 13th Guangdong Provincial Sports Meeting in 1935.

◎幼儿园 Kindergartens

广州是近代较早开展幼儿教育的城市。广州最早的幼儿园成立于清光绪三十三年（1907 年），早期幼儿园称蒙养园，辛亥革命后改称幼稚园。民国时期广州幼稚园大都附设于师范学校、中学幼稚师范班或小学内。创办于 1933 年的广州市立第一幼稚园是广州第一间独立设置的公立幼稚园。民国时期广州各类幼稚园最多时不过 40 所左右，入园幼儿总数最多时只有 3000 多人。

清末广州的蒙养园。当时蒙养园的教师一般由育婴堂、敬节堂的乳媪（即保姆）担任。每日看护幼儿不超过四小时。

A Guangzhou kindergarten in the late Qing Dynasty.At that time, the kindergarten teachers were mainly baby-sitters from nurseries and nurses from old folk's home, who took care of the children for not more than 4 hours a day.

20 世纪 20 年代广州洁芳学校的附属幼稚园。民国时期幼稚园教师多为师范毕业生。

The Kindergarten attached to the Guangzhou Jiefang School in 1920's. During the period of the Republic of China, kindergarten teachers were mainly graduates of normal schools.

刚创办时的广州市立第一幼稚园。园址在惠福东路。当时招收的孩子为4~6岁。幼稚园的课程包括音乐、故事和儿歌、游戏、社会和自然、工作、静息、餐点七项。

The Guangzhou First Kindergarten which was then newly founded an Huifudong Road, recruited children from 4 to 6 years old. In the kindergarten, children learnt music, stories, children's songs, games, society & nature, work, taking break as well as cooking meals.

20世纪30年代初广州私立慈爱幼稚园的孩子们。

The children in the Ciai Private Kindergarten of Guangzhou in early 1930's.

◎广州市立中山图书馆 Municipal Zhongshan Library of Guangzhou

广州市立中山图书馆位于文德路原广府学宫旧址，20 世纪 20 年代后期广州市政府为纪念孙中山先生，向美洲华侨募资 20 余万美元，于 1929 年 12 月动工兴建，1933 年 10 月正式建成。广州沦陷后，该馆停办，抗战胜利后复办。著名学者罗香林、杜定友曾先后担任馆长。1955 年广州市立中山图书馆与广东省立人民图书馆合并后，成为广东省中山图书馆的北馆，1989 年开始称孙中山文献馆。

20 世纪 30 年代新落成的该馆馆舍。外廊仿古宫殿式，内部为西式装饰。

The library building which was then newly built in 1930's. The corridor outside was typical old Chinese palace style, while the interior decoration was all western.

1936 年 12 月该馆全体工作人员合影。

The library staff in December, 1936.

该馆刚建成时的藏书库一角。至 1934 年藏书 98500 余册，报章杂志 200 多种。

One corner of the library when it was first opened to the public. In 1934, the library had 98,500 copies of books and over 200 kinds of magazines and newspapers.

◎流动图书馆 Travelling Libraries

广州市流动图书馆开始出现于民国初年，当时称巡回文库，由广州市督学局创办，1921 年被广州市教育局接管，后隶属广州市第一通俗图书馆。初有箱形和车形两种，雇专人肩挑手推，后增加船形文库，为水上借阅服务。巡回文库设管理员专责办理，将广州市分作若干区，区内又分若干段，分段出巡服务，市民只需填写“借卷”,即可借到 4 册以下的书。后来由于政局动荡，该文库停办。40 年代前期，广州一度又出现过手推车式巡回文库。

20 世纪 20 年代初广州街头的箱形巡回文库。

The street “mobile box library” in Guangzhou in early 1920’s.

20 世纪 20 年代初广州街头的车形巡回文库。

The street "mobile cart library" in Guangzhou in early 1920's.

20 世纪 40 年代初的手推车式巡回文库。

The street "mobile cart library" in Guangzhou in early 1940's.

5 【社会生活】

社会生活是城市永无终结的连续剧。宽阔的舞台，丰富的场景，穿梭其中的芸芸众生扮演着各自不同的角色。他们共同演绎着近代文明社会应有的秩序，凸现的是这个城市最真实的文化内涵。

◎传统功夫 Traditional Kungfu

广州人称武术为“功夫”。近代以来，为了“起民疲、培国脉”，广州练武之风一直很盛。1919 年广东精武体育会在广州海珠戏院成立，1920 年广州还成立了精武童子团，1925 年由河南名士崔鸣舟筹划成立了广州河南精武体育会，1929 年广州国术社成立。武术活动遍及各阶层、各行业。自 1928 年开始，在广州举办的历届省运会中，都有武术比赛。此外，还常有各种武术表演，并举行过擂台赛。至 1949 年，广州约有武馆二三百家。

1922 年 4 月，广东精武体育会举行的大会操上，4 位女童表演拳术。

Four young girls performing Chinese martial art in the Guangdong Jingwu Sports Meeting in April, 1922.

1928年在广东省第十一届运动会上，广州孤儿院学生表演梅花棒。

Guangzhou Orphanage students performing plum stick boxing in the 11th Guangdong Provincial Sports Meeting in 1928.

1928年在广东省第十一届运动会上，元甲女学的学生表演工力拳。

The Yuanjia Girls School students performing craftsmanship boxing in the 11th Guangdong Provincial Sports Meeting in 1928.

1938 年广州国术协会的武术表演。

Martial art performance in the Guangzhou Chinese Martial Art Assciation in 1938.

1933 年在广东省第十二届运动会上，广州体专的谭文彪进行汽车过腹的气功表演。

Qigong performance of a car going over human stomach by Tan Wenbiao from the Guangzhou Junior College of Sports in the 12th Guangdong Provincial Sports Meeting in 1933.

◎健身操　Body-building Exercise

近代体育从欧美和日本传入中国，广东颇得风气之先。广州徒手体操运动最早出现于19世纪七八十年代的教会学校及官立军事学堂。之后各类新式学堂纷纷开设体操课，主要是兵式健身操。直到1923年国民政府颁布新学制标准，才将体操课改为体育课，但徒手操一直是各类学校最基本的一项集体体育活动。

20世纪20年代初广州洁芳学校的学生在做健身操。当时体操课是小学生的必修课。

In early 1920's, Guangzhou Jiefang School students are doing body-building exercise, which was at that time a required course for primary students.

1933年广东国民大学的学生在做早操。

Students of Guangdong National University doing morning exercise in 1933.

1940 年广州小学生做健身操。

Guangzhou primary students doing body-building exercise in 1940.

1951 年广州幼儿园的孩子做操的场面。

Guangzhou kindergarten children doing body exercise in 1951.

◎女子体育　Girl's Physical Education

自清末广州女性取得接受学校教育的机会，女子体育运动也随之起步。1912年广东最早的体育学校——私立广东女子体育学校在广州成立，主要培养小学体育师资。随着女子体育运动的振兴，广州涌现了一批优秀女运动员。自1930年起，以广州运动员为主的广东女子排球队、广东女子田径队、广东女子垒球队和广东女子游泳队在数届全国运动会上先后夺冠。

1912年在广东男女学生运动会上，女子撑伞竞走比赛的场面。

Girl's race with an open umbrella in the Guangdong Boy & Girl Students Sports Meeting in 1912.

1923年广州洁芳学校的学生在打排球。

Students of the Guangzhou Jiefang School playing volleyball in 1923.

1933年执信女子中学的排球队员。当时的体育课，初中每周3小时，高中每周2小时，课外活动每天至少半小时。

Volleyball players of the Zhixin Girl's Secondary School in 1933. At that time, students in junior middle school had 3 hours of P.E. and those in the senior had 2 hours of P.E. every week, and both had half an hour's extracurricular activities.

1935年广东省立女子师范学校的学生在跨栏比赛中。

Students of Guangdong Girl's Normal School having hurdle race in 1935.

女学生之二人三足竞走。

The girl students in the three-legged-heel-to-toe walking race.

◎广州市第一次自行车长途赛 The First Bicycle Race of Long-Distance in Guangzhou

自行车，又称脚踏车或单车，20 世纪初已出现在广州街头。据不完全统计，1928 年，广州市区共有自行车 2600 余辆，1948 年达 2 万多辆。除用作交通外，骑自行车也是一种健身运动。在 1917 年第七届广东省运动会的田径项目中已有了自行车比赛，参赛者全是广州选手。1930 年夏，广州市在番花公路举办了第一次自行车长途赛。

运动员准备出发的场面。

Cyclists get ready to start the competition.

此次比赛的第一名黎文汉，第二名佘福生。

In the competition, Li Wenhan got the first, and She Fusheng the second.

比赛结束后，广东省建设厅厅长邓彦华（中穿西服者）与全体参赛者的合影。

After the competition, Deng Yanhua, director of the Guangdong Provincial Construction Department (the man in a suit standing in the middle) had this group photo taken to mark the occasion.

◎环市长跑 Long-distant Race Around the City

广州自清末起，有了长跑运动项目。20 世纪 30 年代广州市共举办了 8 次环市长跑赛。比赛设有严密的组织机构，制定有详细的比赛规则，凡年龄 16 岁以上，不拘性别、职业、国籍均可报名，仅 1936 年和 1937 年两次环市长跑赛单为男子参加。20 世纪 40 年代广州市也组织过多次环市长跑赛。

1933 年广州市举行第四次环市长跑赛。图为赛前运动员静听宣布比赛规则。

Sportsmen attentively listening to race rules before the 4th Round-the-City Race held in Guangzhou in 1933.

比赛开始时全体运动员在东较场体育场绕场跑一周。

All sportsmen running for one circle around the Dongjiaochang palyground at the beginning of the race.

这次环市长跑赛女子组的优胜者。第一名冯景炘来自体育学校。

The champion of the girl's group in the Round-the-City Race.Feng Jingxin, who got the first place, came from a sports school.

1942 年广州市环市长跑赛的场面。

The Guangzhou Round-the-City Race in 1942.

◎省运会　Provincial Sports Meeting

广东省举办省运会始于清光绪三十一年（1906 年）冬。晚清和民国时期，广东共举行过 15 届省运会，地点均在广州，参赛单位大都是广州市内各学校。从 1921 年第八届省运会开始，广州市郊县学校和香港一些学校、社团也来穗参赛。在历次省运会中，广州市的岭南大学、南武学堂、省立女师、中山大学、省立体育专科学校、培正中学等校选手曾有较突出的表现。

1906 年广东省第一次运动大会的一个场景：运动员将至终点，评判员走入跑道以迎接前三名，并陪跑到终点线。

The 1st Guangdong Provincial Sports Meeting in 1906 sportsmen are coming to the finishing line, and judges are going to the track to greet the first 3 runners and to accompany them to the finishing tape.

清光绪三十二年（1907年）第二届省运会的会场。

The 2nd Guangdong Provincial Sports Meeting in 1907 (the 32rd year of Emperor Guangxu of the Qing Dynasty) .

1933年第十二届省运会的会场主席台。

The rostrum of the 12th Guangdong Provincial Sports Meeting in 1933.

1937 年第十四届省运会女子甲组四百米接力赛的决赛场面。

Girl's Class A finals of the 400-metre relay race in the 14th Provincial Sports Meeting in 1937.

◎博济医院 The Boji Hospital

近代以来，西方人在来华传教的同时也带来了西医。博济医院原是美国传教医生伯驾于清道光十五年（1835 年）创办的眼科医局。它是外国教会在中国内地开设的第一间教会医院，也是中国第一间西医医院。清咸丰五年（1855 年）该院由广州医学传道会接办。原址在广州十三行，咸丰六年（1856 年）因火灾停办。咸丰九年(1859 年)于广州增沙街(今南关)复办。清同治五年（1866 年）迁至仁济大街(孙逸仙纪念医院现址)，改名博济医院。该院当时实施的很多手术都属中国内地首创。1930 年，博济医院移交岭南大学办理，该院遂成为岭南大学医学院的附属医院，原岭南大学附属医院改为博济分院。日占时期，博济医院院址曾一度被日本博爱会医院霸占，抗战胜利后恢复。新中国成立后，该院先后改名华南医学院第二附属医院和中山医学院第二附属医院。1985 年正式称中山医科大学孙逸仙纪念医院。

1934 年博济医院前门。

The front gate of the Boji Hospital in 1934.

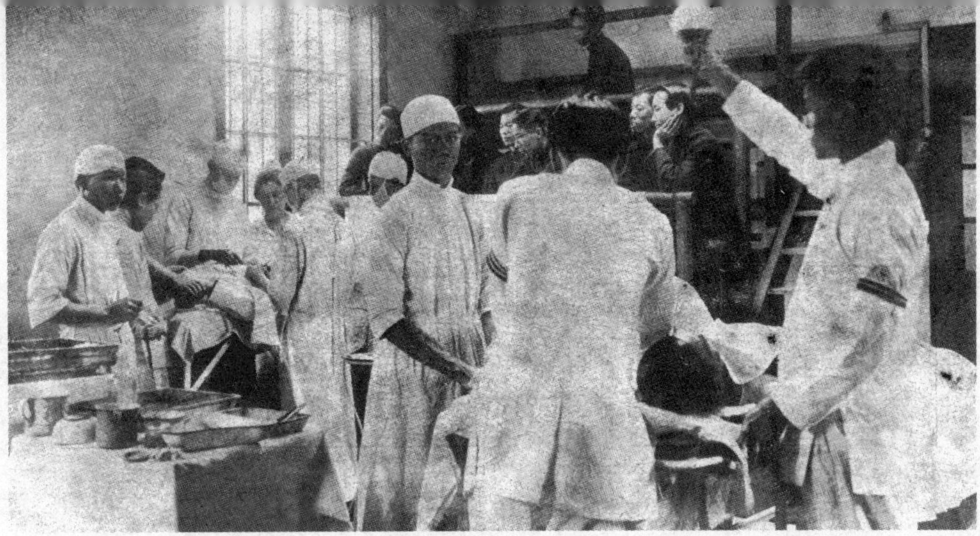

1917 年该院手术室和病房。该院擅长外科手术，至 1935 年，该院共施行外科手术 20 多万人次，占治疗病人总数的十分之一。

The operating room and ward of the hospital in 1917.The hospital is famous for surgical operations.By the end of 1935, 200, 200 cases of surgical operations had been done here, which accounts for 10 percent of the total number of the patients of the hospital.

1917年该院全体医护人员合影。

The staff of the hospital in 1917.

◎广州方便医院　Guangzhou Fangbian Hospital

广州方便医院前身是清光绪二十五年（1899 年）建立的城西方便所，不久与城北方便所合并，称广州城西方便医院。该院依靠穗、港、澳绅商募集捐款，主要收治那些无力问医的病者，为当时华南最大的慈善机构，也是广东第一间较具规模的中医医院。1926 年，方便医院开始兼设西医，成为当时广东唯一中西医兼备的医院。其后，该院逐步以西医药治疗为主。1949 年 1 月该院正式称广州方便医院。1953 年，该院与广州市市立医院合并为广州市人民医院，1954 年起称广州市第一人民医院。

20 世纪 20 年代该院大门。

The hospital gate in 1920's.

20世纪20年代后期该院救护队和药房。

The hospital ambulance and pharmacy in late 1920's.

◎广州市市立医院　Guangzhou Municipal Hospital

广州市市立医院的前身是1912年创办于南堤（今沿江中路）的警察医院，1917年改名广东医院，迁院址至九曜坊（今教育路西湖路口）。1921年改名为广州市市立医院。1931年再迁至盘福路。1936年市立医院接收广东仁爱医院，改组为广州市市立医院第一分院。日占时期，市立医院及其分院均停办，1946年复办。新中国成立后，广州市市立医院与广州方便医院合并为广州市人民医院，1954年改名为广州市第一人民医院。

1935年该院大门。

The hospital gate in 1935.

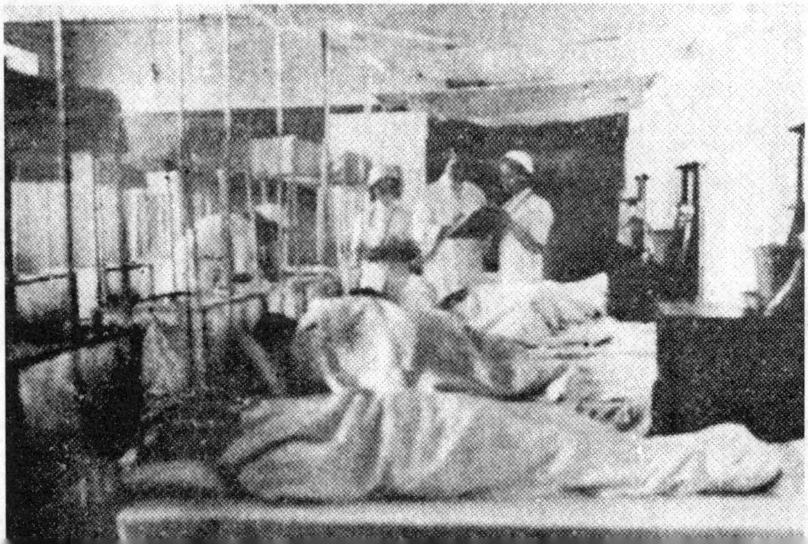

20世纪30年代该院妇科留产室。当时该院医务分内、外、儿妇、产、眼耳鼻喉、皮肤及X光电疗7科。

Department of Gynaecology and Obstetrics of the hospital in 1930's.At that time, there were all together 7 departments in the hospital——the medical, the surgical, the women & infants, the obstetrics, the ophthalmology & otolaryngology, the dermatology and the X-ray electrotherapy.

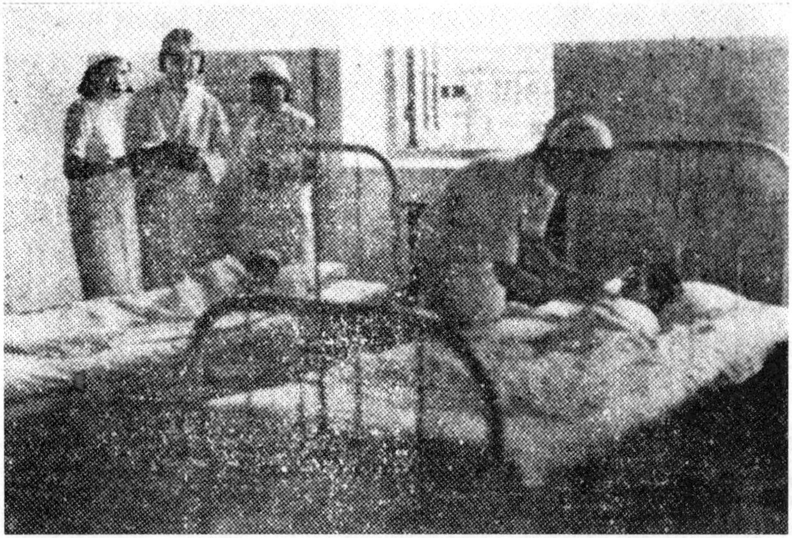

该院儿科病房。

The infants chinic ward of the hospital.

1934年的广州市市立医院。

The Guangzhou Municipal Hospital in 1934.

◎影戏院　Movie Theaters

电影于 20 世纪初从国外传入广州。当时被称作电影戏、影画戏等。早期放映的电影都是无声电影，有解画员同步讲解，广州人称为“默片”。1930 年，广州开始出现有声电影。最初的电影放映只是零星的和临时性的，后来逐渐出现营业性的放映场所，被称作影戏院或影画院。广州首家影戏院为镜花台影戏院。自清末至 20 世纪 40 年代末，广州市先后开办的影戏院将近 60 家。广州解放前夕，市区公开营业的影戏院和其他放映单位共 25 个。

1921 年建成的明珠影画院，位于长堤。它是无声电影时期广州规模最大、设备最好的影戏院。座位分为三等。前、中座是男座，女座分居两侧，包厢男女同坐。座位背后有长板，中有圆空，可放茶盅。

The Pearl Cinema at Changdi of Guangzhou was built in 1921.It was the largest scale cinema with the best facilities in Guangzhou during the period of silent movies.The seats were separated into 3 classes, the front and the centre were for men, while women were on both sides.Boxes were for both men and women.Behind each seat, there was a board, the centre of which was a circular hole big enough for a tea cup.

位于永汉路(今北京路)和文明路交界的永汉影戏院，1927年建成。

The Yonghan Theatre, built in 1927, was at the juncture of Yonghan Road (now Beijing Road) and Wenming Road.

位于惠爱中路(今中山五路)的新华戏院，1933年建成。

The Sunwah Theatre, built in 1933, was at Huiaizhong Road (now Zhongshanwu Road) .

◎粤剧和粤曲 Canton Opera & Canton Folk Music

粤剧已有300多年历史，是广东最大的地方戏曲剧种，广州是粤剧发源地之一。辛亥革命前后，广州出现了粤剧改良运动，古装与时装并举，粤剧与话剧相结合。20世纪20年代初，粤剧完成了平喉代替假嗓，全部改用广州方言演唱的声腔革命及语言、板式结构、曲调等重大变革。此后又有精简行当、丰富唱腔音乐、引入外国乐器等革新，使粤剧逐步成为现代粤剧。粤曲原为粤剧的曲调，后形成独立曲种，是广东最大的地方曲种，约有150年历史。

20世纪三四十年代广州粤剧演出的舞台场景。

Canton opera being performed in Guang-zhou during 1930's and 1940's.

20世纪30年代末广州粤剧演出的舞台场景。

Canton opera being performed in Guangzhou in 1930's.

20世纪40年代初广州女学生演唱粤曲的场面。伴奏的乐队既有小提琴、电吉他，又有扬琴、月琴等。

A Guangzhou girl student singing Cantonese songs in 1940's, accompanied by a band of violin, electric guitar, dulcimer and Chinese four-stringed full-moon-shaped lute etc.

◎黄包车　Rickshaws

黄包车也叫手拉车，是旧时代城市街道上最具代表性的一道风景。19 世纪末 20 世纪初传入广州，俗称“手车”或“车仔”。20 世纪二三十年代，随着广州市大规模辟建马路，黄包车被大量购进，成为广州市区最常见的客运交通工具。20 世纪 30 年代中期,手车多达 5600 多辆，私人自用的 200 辆左右,其余由安乐、普达、安平、利昌、恒益、广利 6 家公司经营，而以此为业的黄包车车夫总数达 5253 名。抗战胜利后，广州市人力脚踏三轮车行业开始崛起，黄包车行业逐渐没落。到广州解放前夕，广州市还有黄包车 900 辆。1956 年 3 月，广州市最后 4 辆黄包车也停止了营运。

20 世纪三四十年代广州街头的黄包车。

The Guangzhou street rickshaws during 1930's and 1940's.

20 世纪 30 年代四牌楼前的黄包车。

The rickshaws before the Four Memorial Stone Archways in 1930's.

20 世纪 30 年代初靖海路上的黄包车。

The rickshaws on Jinghai Road in early 1930's.

◎公共汽车　Buses

1920年，广州街头开始出现客运汽车。1926年，广州市政当局招商5家公司承办客运汽车业务，共有汽车30辆。1928年广州市公用局开办了市营搭客汽车，每辆可载乘客30人左右，路线一条，由财厅前经双门底（今北京路）右转长堤到沙基，终点站黄沙。1934年广州市区共有搭客汽车线路14条。1936年广州公共汽车正式得名。1937年广州10家小公司合组公共汽车股份有限公司，共有公共汽车166辆。广州解放前夕，广州共有公共汽车240辆，全部为私营，行驶16条线路，车辆及所需配件、油料完全依赖进口。

20世纪20年代末广州街头的公共汽车。当时的搭客汽车多为24座，是广州市公用局在香港订造的，车上装有弹簧座位，并设电灯、电铃，乘客上下车可按电铃通知司机停车、开车。

Guangzhou buses in late 1920's.At that time, most passenger buses, which were all made to order in Hong Kong by the Guangzhou Public Utility Department, had 24 spring seats with lights and bells.Passengers told the driver where to stop by pressing the electric bell.

20世纪20年代末广州市营长途汽车、电单车队和广州市公用局职员。

Staff of the Guangzhou Public Utility Department and the city-run coaches and motorcycles in late 1920's.

◎交通岗亭 Traffic boxes

扩马路、通汽车后，广州的街头才出现了交通指挥。它最早始于 1918 年，由交通警察手持黑白相间的指挥棍站在路口中央指挥车辆。1928 年，广州市区 22 个路口都设立了较完备的交通指挥岗亭。到广州解放前夕，全市还有残旧的交通岗台约 100 个，有红绿灯设备的只占 10%。

20 世纪 20 年代广州街头的交通岗。

The traffic post in a Guangzhou street in 1920's.

20世纪20年代末的广州交通岗亭。岗亭最上面是5头电灯，其下为大挂钟，再下面为交通红绿灯和交警岗位篷盖。

The street traffic post in Guangzhou in late 1920's.On the top of the post were 5 electric lamps.A big clock was under the lamps.The traffic lights and a loose lid were just below the clock.

20 世纪 40 年代初广州惠爱中路（今中山五路）的交通岗一景。

The traffic post on Huiaizhong Road (now Zhongshanwu Road) in early 1940's.

◎火车 Trains

火车是交通现代化的一个标志。清光绪二十九年（1903 年），广三线建成，以石围塘为始发站。清宣统三年（1911 年）广九线通车，在大沙头设客运站。1916 年粤汉铁路广韶线运营，始发站为黄沙。1938 年粤汉铁路与广九铁路在广州石牌接轨。1947 年广九、粤汉铁路的旅客列车均以大沙头为起止站，大沙头改名广州东站，专营客运；黄沙站更名广州南站，主营列车编组和货运。民国时期广州铁路运输设备均购自欧美国家。

1931 年大沙头车站外景。

The Dashatou Bus Station in 1931.

1928年广九铁路列车抵达广州大沙头站的情景。

The Canton-Kowloon train arriving at Dashatou, Guangzhou in 1928.

1934年粤汉铁路广州黄沙车站。

Guangzhou Huangsha Train Station of the Canton-Hankou Railway in 1934.

1937 年广九铁路管理局
“曙光”号的冷气车厢。

Air-conditioned railway carriages of the train “Dawn” run by the Canton-Kowloon Railroad Administration in 1937.

◎轮渡 Ferries

早先，广州珠江两岸的水上交通仅依靠木质横水渡和沙艇，横水渡每艘可载客6～8人，沙艇每艘可载2～3人，均属私营船只。直到1921年，广州市才开始有机动渡轮往来珠江水面。机动渡轮为木质电船，每艘载客不超过60人，最初为招商承运，其后经历过官督商办、官办、商办等多种方式。但整个民国时期最主要的渡江交通工具始终是横水渡。

20世纪30年代初的广州渡船。当时规定的过江时间是早上4时至深夜12时。

Guangzhou ferry in early 1930's.At that time, the ferry hour is 4 A.M to 12 P.M.

清末珠江上的木渡船。

The wooden ferries on the Pearl River in the Late Qing Dynasty.

20世纪40年代初的广州轮渡。

Guangzhou ferry in 1940's.

轮渡上配备的小土炮，用于防卫江面上的土匪。

The homemade cannons set on the ferry, were used to de fend against the bandits on the river.

◎花舫 The Recreation Boats

花舫也称“紫洞艇”，是一种装饰华丽的大型游船，它始于明代，原为妓艇，清刘叙堂在《粤游笔记》中说：“珠江花船，甲于天下，有苏扬、本地各帮之号。所居楼船，名之为寮，一寮贮百余妓，比屋分房，形如鸽笼。中有公堂，铺设华丽，供奉财神……床帐字画，靡不精细，灯盆镜奁，无一不齐。”后以酒席饮宴为主。民国时期花舫仍很盛行。花舫分两种，一种固定停泊于东堤一带，专供人们宴饮，相当于酒舫。另一种供人们租用，既可游河，又可在舫内宴饮。20 世纪 40 年代后期，花舫逐渐消失。

花舫船舱用上等木材和嵌花玻璃隔成厅房，垂着珠帘，五光十色，内置酸枝云石台椅，布置豪华，船头还围着朱漆栏杆。大的花舫有两层，设几个大厅，可摆 10 多桌酒席。图为清末广州的花舫。

The “Flower Boat” (recreation boat) cabin is usually separated into a sitting room and bedrooms by superior wood and flower-pattern-inlaid glass, and decorated with color-ful pearl curtains and fine padauk teak mar-ble tables and chairs.The stem is encircled by red painted rails.A big “Flower Boat” has 2 storeys with several separated halls large enough for ten-odd banquet tables.The typical “Flower Boat” in Guangzhou in the late Qing Dynasty.

20世纪30年代初的珠江花舫泊满了长堤和黄沙一带的河面。

A lot of "Flower Boats" anchored alongside the Pearl River shore of Changdi and Huangsha in early 1930's.

◎水浸街　Streets Flooded by River Water

广州地处珠江三角洲北端三江汇流处，珠江穿市而过，西北紧靠流溪河，北临北江，雨量充沛，暴雨集中，因而备受洪水、暴雨、大潮威胁，历史上洪涝灾害频繁。近百年来广州最大的一次洪灾发生在1915年夏，由于北江溃决，洪水倾泻，广州城区尤其沿江一带悉成泽国，造成民居崩塌，伤亡无数，史称“乙卯水灾”。1932年夏，广州暴雨，白云山山洪突发，小北首当其冲，汪洋一片，再次酿成屋塌人亡的惨剧。此外，1947年夏的大洪水也使广州及邻近各县普遍受灾，程度仅次于乙卯年。

1915年夏广州长堤水灾情形。

The flood in Changdi of Guangzhou in 1915.

1915年夏广州市区部分街道的水灾情景。“落雨大、水浸街……”这一民谣已经成为昔日粤人生活的一个注解。

The flood in some streets in the urban area of Guangzhou in 1915. “Once it rains hard, the streets get flooded…” This folk rhyme reflects the life of Guangzhou people at that time.

1932年夏广州小北一带的水浸情形。

The flood at the area of Xiaobei Road of Guangzhou in 1932.

1948 年 9 月一场暴雨过后，广州沿江路一带水浸的情形。

Yanjiang Road of Guangzhou was flooded after a rain storm in September, 1948.

◎消防 Fire fighting

清光绪二十九年（1903 年），广州始设消防所，位于三府前（今海珠南），隶属广东巡警总局，不久又设第一、第二、第三消防分所。早期灭火全靠人力，人们排起长队，从火场到水源处一盆一桶传递泼救。1921 年，广州开始从国外购进专业灭火器械，同时，广州市公安局消防所扩为消防总所，先迁连新路，后迁至文明路。又相继设立第四、第五、第六消防分所以及水上消防分所。此外，还有下九甫联合救火会、各街坊义勇消防队等救火团体。1938 年广州消防警察共有 300 余名，连同民间消防队员逾千名。广州解放前夕，广州警察局消防总队有消防车 10 台，义勇消防队有消防车 15 台。

1922 年广州市消防警察演习的场面。

The Guangzhou Fire Brigade having fire drills in 1922.

1923 年广州下九甫联合救火会的义务救火队员。

The volunteer firemen of the Xiajiufu United Fire Association of Guangzhou in 1923.

20 世纪 30 年代文明路的广州市公安局消防总所。

The Headquarter of the Fire Department of Guangzhou Police Station on Wenming Road in 1930's.

1948 年广州市汉民区的义勇消防队员。

The firemen of the Hanmin District Fire Department of Guangzhou in 1948.

◎环卫 Environmental Sanitation

广州市环境卫生由政府实施行政管理，始于清光绪二十九年（1903 年）广东巡警总局设立卫生科，开始雇用清洁夫打扫街道，清运垃圾。1921 年这项工作改由卫生局接管。1927 年广州全市共有清洁夫 1200 多名。1930 年广州市卫生局又成立清理股，专司清粪管理工作。到广州解放前夕，广州市共有垃圾汽车 5 辆，粪溺汽车 7 辆，洒水车 2 辆。新中国成立后，广州市政府加强环境卫生管理，使广州市容环境卫生面貌有了很大改观。1990 年广州共有环卫职工 12479 人，拥有各种环卫车辆 558 辆，基本实现了垃圾、粪便收集容器化，装卸自动或半自动化，清运机械化，处理无害化。

20 世纪 30 年代广州市卫生局管理的粪车。当时广州按繁盛区和僻静区、夏秋季和冬春季规定不同清粪时间。清粪夫则分倒粪工、担粪工、车面工。

The dung-carts of the Guangzhou Health Department in 1930's.At that time, Guangzhou had different night soil clearing time for different districts and different seasons of the year.The workers included loading men, carrying men and men working on carts.

1936年广州市政府派人督责市民做好环境清洁卫生。

Officials of Guangzhou City Government supervising and directing enviromental cleaning in 1936.

20 世纪 30 年代广州市卫生局的清洁洗射队。

The Cleaning Brigade of the Guangzhou Health Department in 1930's.

1937 年广州市夏令卫生运动中清洁队的旗帜和垃圾车。

Flags and rubbish carts of the Cleaning Brigade during the Guangzhou Summer Hygien Movement in 1937.

◎彩牌楼 The Decorated Archways

清末和民国时期，在广州一些大的集会、游行、庆典活动中，常会出现一种标志性门楼式建筑，广州人多称之为彩牌楼或牌楼。它通常是竹木结构的临时建筑，或两柱单间，或四柱三间，门楼层数不等，高的可达7层，10多丈高，配上色彩缤纷的竹席，堪称一座艺术造型。牌楼通常耸立在集会入口处或街口，十分醒目，起到广而告之的作用。

1931年广州纪念“五四运动”的牌楼。

The Ceremonial gateway commemorating the May 4th Movement.

1931年1月在丰宁路（今人民中路）举行广州市国货展览会的牌楼。

The decorated gateway on Fengning Road (now Renminzhong Road) of the Guangzhou National Products Fair in January, 1931.

1933年2月在粤秀山举办广州第一次展览会的牌楼。

The decorated gateway of the 1st Guangzhou Exhibition Fair held at Yuexiu Hill in February, 1933.

1950年10月广州市庆祝解放一周年的牌楼。

The decorated gafeway of Guangzhou City celebrationg the anniversary of liberation in October, 1950.

◎人口调查　Population Cenaus

历史上的人口统计都是通过户籍管理来进行的。20 世纪初广东建立警政，户口管理与调查由警察机构负责。民国成立后，广州市拆城辟路，市辖区域发生很大变化，流动人口激增，居无定所者为数甚多。广州市政府遂于 1932 年进行了一次大规模人口调查，前后历时 5 个月，机关职员、大中学校学生和教职员等近 2 万余人参加了这次调查工作。调查结果，广州市区人口达 104.26 万人，首次突破百万。这是广州历史上第一次大规模的人口普查活动。

1932 年广州市人口调查活动的宣传标语。

Population census posters in Guangzhou City in 1932.

调查人员集合起来，准备出发收集调查表格的场面。

Census investigating workers getting together to set off and collect the questionnaires.

调查员上门查访的情景。

Census investigating workers making door–to–door inquiries.

6 【民生习俗】

民生习俗是市井的万花筒。衣食住行，无论粗重还是浮华，都联结着民众最基本的生活需求。而四时的节日，人生的典礼，种种悲喜忧欢，无不折射出这个城市最真实的表情。

◎男装 Men's Clothing

清末和民国时期广州男性服装既有大襟衫（也称长袍）、马褂、唐装等传统服饰，也流行中山装和西装等“文明装”。民国时期，广州地区公务人员多穿中山装、西装；工商界人士多着西装、便服、长衫；青年学生则穿企领文装、衬衫、西裤。

清末广州帮办洋务的翻译。

Interpreters of Guangzhou Foreign Affairs Department in the late Qing Dynasty.

清末广州的读书人，后两排皆穿无领长衫，前排3位着立领学生装。

Guangzhou students in the late Qing Dynasty.Students at the last 2 rows wear long gowns without a collar, while those at the first row wear collared students uniform.

民国初年的广州青年学生，服装亦中亦西。

Guangzhou students in the early period of the Republic of China wear both Chinese traditional and western style costumes.

20世纪30年代广州的中学教师，以西装为主。
Guangzhou middle school teachers in 1930's mostly wear suits.

◎女装 Women's Clothing

清末和民国时期，广州女性服装主要有旗袍、唐装衫裤、大襟衫以及西装衣裙等。清代旗袍是直筒式，腰部无曲线，下摆和袖口较大，宽袖无领，袖边、领口和衣襟有镶边。民国时期的旗袍多高领，胸襟较宽松，腰围微紧，下摆开衩。衣身长短不定，袖子长短宽紧不一。民国时期女学生常穿长衫或短衫、裙子等。

清末广州的贵妇。

A Guangzhou noble lady in the late Qing Dynasty.

清末广州普通妇女。

Guangzhou common women in the late Qing Dynasty.

20世纪20年代的广州女子。

A Guangzhou lady in 1920's.

20世纪30年代广州的女职员。

Women clerks in Guangzhou in 1930's.

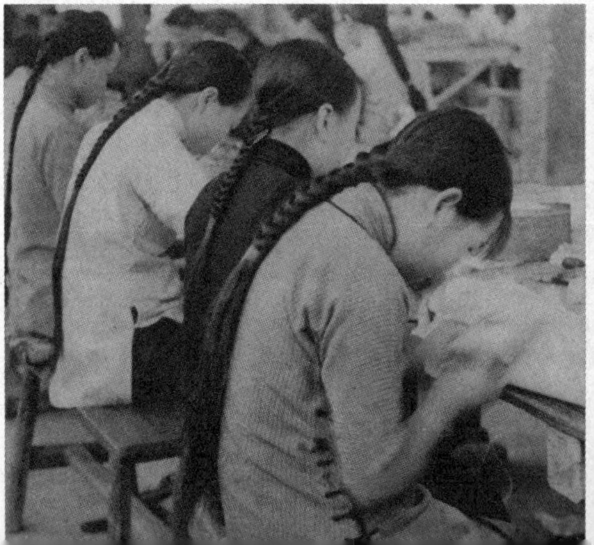

20世纪40年代初广州的女缝工，穿短大襟，梳长辫子。

Women tailors in Guangzhou in early 1940's wear short garments and usually wear their hair in long braids.

◎苦力 Coolie

民国时期，广州的苦力在全市职业人口中占据较大比例。据1928年4月的统计，当时广州的苦力工人有35694人。广州苦力通常穿唐装衫裤或大襟短衫。大襟短衫为平日劳动的便装，是靛蓝或藏青色的粗陋布衣。

20世纪30年代广州的挑担夫。

A coolie in Guangzhou in 1930's.

20 世纪 40 年代初广州的搬运苦力。旧时广州称搬运工为“咕哩”。

Porters and dockers in Guangzhou in early 1940's were usually called “Guli” (“coolie”) .

◎老人　Old People

1911 年广州 65 岁以上的老人有 1.6 万人，占总人口 3.1%。1936 年有 4.5 万人，占总人口 3.9%。1949 年降至 2.8 万人，仅占总人口 1.98%。1929 年，广州市人口平均预期寿命为 35 岁，男性 37.8 岁，女性 32.5 岁。1947 年广州人口平均预期寿命升至 48.3 岁，其中男性 47.7 岁，女性 48.9 岁。

1933 年 2 月 1 日，出席广州市政府举行耆英大会的两位广州百岁老人。

Two of the hundred-year-old people attended the conference of Respecting the Aged held in Guangzhou on Feb. 1st, 1933.

出席耆英大会的广州老人伍黎鸿福，她 90 岁，有子孙 57 人，为五代同堂。即在当时，也是凤毛麟角。

Mrs. Wu Li Hongfu, a 90-year old Guangzhou old woman, attended the conference of Respecting the Aged.She was then blessed with 5 generations of totally 57 descendants, which was quite rare at that period of time.

20世纪20年代末伏案挥笔的广州老人。

An old man bends over his desk writing in Guangzhou in 1920's.

1934年，广州106岁老人张苏氏在穿针刺绣。

Ms.Zhang Su, aged 106, embroidering in Guangzhou in 1934.

20 世纪 30 年代广州旧凤凰村的老人。

Old people living in Jiufenghuang Village of Guangzhou in 1930's.

◎少儿 Children

少儿人口指 0～14 岁人口。依照 1911 年的有关资料，当时广州少儿人口有 11.44 万人，占总人口 22.09%。民国成立后，少儿人口比重起伏不定，但基本呈上升趋势。民国期间广州学龄儿童入学率低，启蒙教育发展曲折。1928 年广州学龄儿童入学率为 78.95%，1932 年为 52.97%，1946 年为 50.30%。

清末广州贫民的孩子，衣不蔽体。

Children of the poor people in Guangzhou wearing shabby clothes in the late Qing Dynasty.

20 世纪 30 年代广州旧凤凰村的学童。

Pupils of Jiufenghuang Village of Guangzhou in 1930's.

1932 年广州四对双胞胎。

A photo of 4 pairs of twins in Guangzhou in 1932.

1935 年广州中上阶层家庭的孩子。

Children from the mid-upper class families in Guangzhou in 1935.

◎母婴 Mothers and Babies

近代以前，广州妇女分娩都由产婆接产，用瓷片断脐，没有消毒设施，产妇生命没有保障。广州俗语称“生仔如见阎罗王——隔张纸”，婴儿死亡率很高。清末博济医院妇女部及柔济女医院建立后，开始有了科学的接生方法。但由于社会不稳定，生活水平低下，土法接生仍大量存在。1928年广州婴儿死亡率高达55.5%，到1948年，婴儿死亡率仍在10%左右。

1915年广州一位年轻母亲与她刚满百日的婴儿的合影。

A young mother and her 100-day-old baby in Guangzhou in 1915.

20世纪30年代初期广州几位初为人母的妇女与她们的新生儿。

Some young mothers and their new-born babies in Guangzhou in early 1930's.

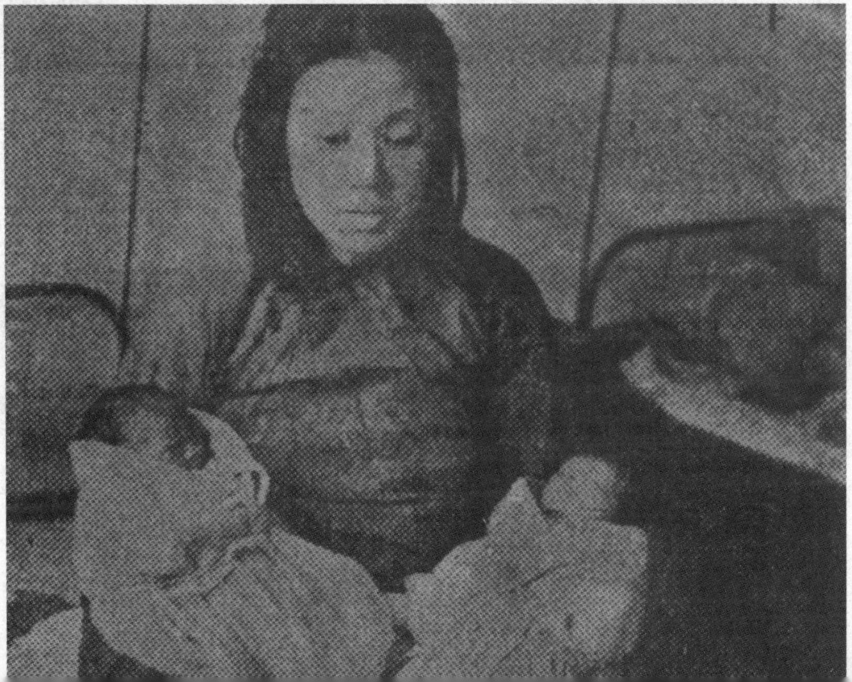

1946年广州一位产妇与她的一对孪生子。

A lying-in woman and her twin sons in Guangzhou in 1946.

◎食在广州 Eating in Guangzhou

清末和民国时期，广州的饮食业十分繁盛。茶楼、酒家、茶室、饭店、包办馆、西餐馆、冰室、粉面馆、小食店（担）、茶寮、紫洞艇、花酌馆等星罗棋布，饮食品种丰富多彩，制作精良考究，形成兼纳中西、融汇南北的特色，赢得“食在广州”的美誉。

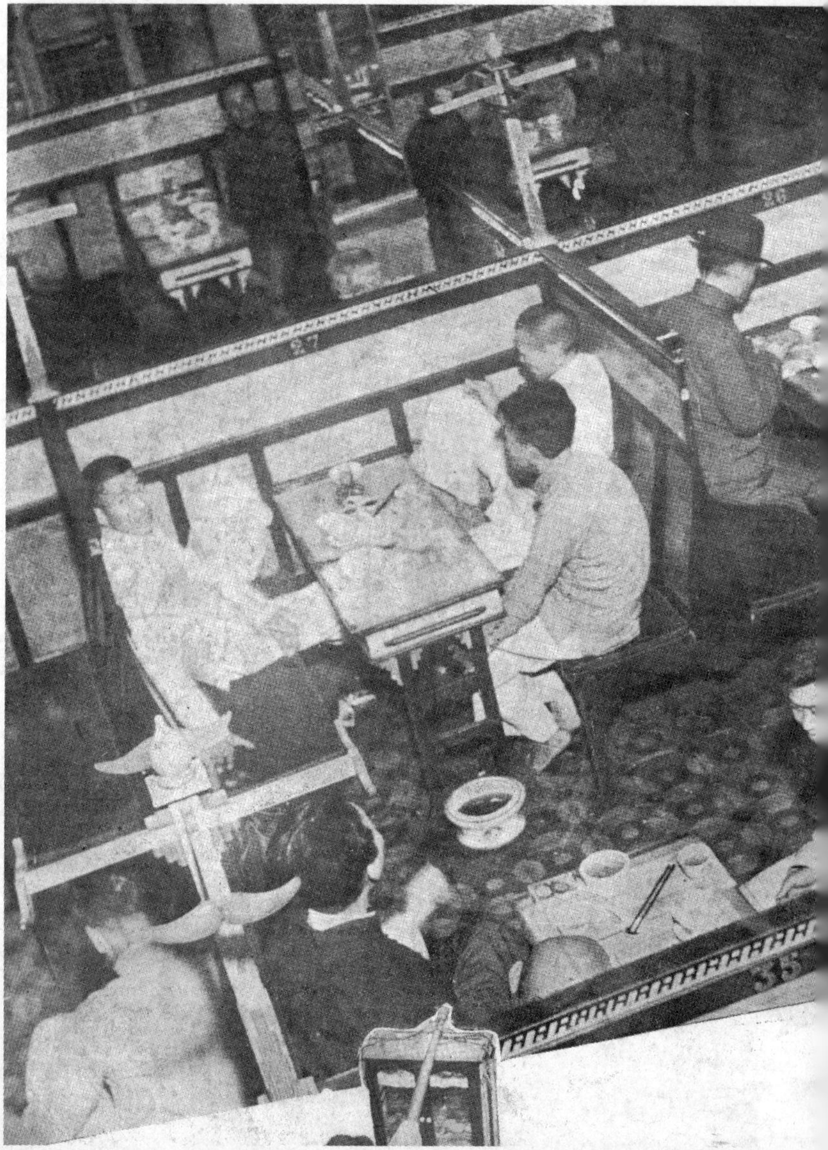

20世纪三四十年代广州茶楼内景。

The interior of Guangzhou teahouses during 1930's and 1940's.

20 世纪 40 年代初广州酒楼的女食客。

Women customers of a Guangzhou teahouse in early 1940's.

1949 年广州街边的小食店，主顾多是车夫和小贩。

A Guangzhou sidewalk snack eatery in 1949, whose customers are mainly carters and pedlars.

20世纪50年代初广州荔湾湖上卖艇仔粥的小艇。艇仔粥通常以新鲜的鱼片或河虾作配料，并添加海蜇、炒花生仁、浮皮、葱花、姜等，吃前当即煮粥滚制，鲜甜香美，深受人们欢迎，是广州特有的粥品。

The small boat selling Tingzai Porridge on the Liwan Lake of Guangzhou in 1950's.The mix ingredients of such porridge are usually fresh fish slice or river shrimps, together with jellyfish, fried peanut, fried flour flake, chopped green onion and ginger efc.This typical and popular Cantonese porridge is fresh and delicious because it is often instantly cooked just before served.

◎茶楼　Teahouse

清末，广州开始出现茶居，即档次较高的茶馆，后来有了楼高3层的茶居，始称茶楼。“有钱楼上楼，无钱地下踎”，饮茶风尚遍及各阶层。茶楼多设在人烟稠密的商业区和交通要道，大、中型茶楼注重门面装修，布置古色古香。营业分早、午、晚三个茶市，一般以早茶为主。除茶市供应外，茶楼还兼做中秋、春节、端午等节令的饼食供应。从20世纪40年代中期开始，一些大茶楼迫于竞争，兼营酒菜筵席，成为茶市、饭市、酒菜筵席综合经营的饮食店，形成“三茶两饭”的经营特点。广州著名的老茶楼有陆羽居、陶陶居、莲香楼、惠如楼、涎香楼、南如楼等。“米珠薪桂了无惊，装饰奢华饮食精。绝似升平歌舞日，茶楼处处管弦声。”茶楼由此而成了广州饮食繁盛的代表。

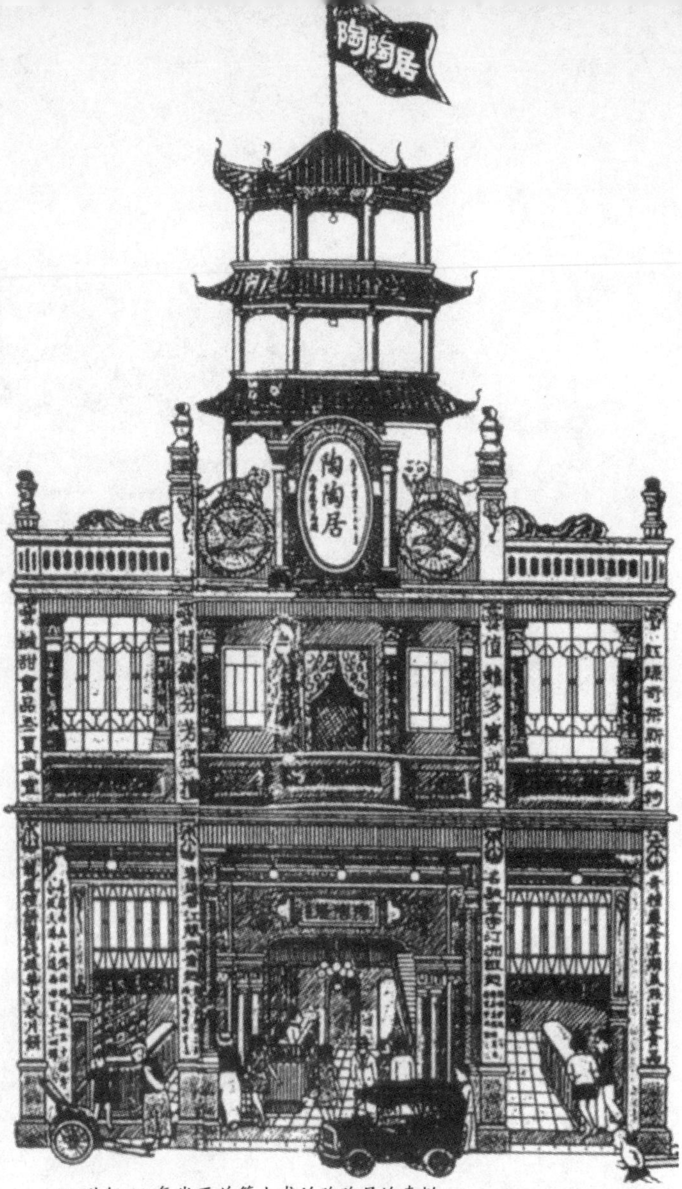

20世纪30年代西关第十甫的陶陶居的素描。

A sketch of the Taotaoju Teahouse at Dishifu of Xiguan, Guangzhou, in 1930’s.

20世纪30年代广州河南的高升大茶楼门前。

The Gaosheng Teahouse at Henan of Guangzhou in 1930's.

20世纪40年代位于西关第十甫的莲香楼。

The Lianxiang Teahouse at Dishifu of Xiguan of Guangzhou in 1940's.

◎西关大屋和竹筒屋 Traditional Xiguan Big Houses & Bamboo Tube Houses

西关大屋出现于清中叶以后，是广州望族、官僚、商贾在西关兴建的具有广州特色的大屋。一般为三间两廊，二三进深，砖木结构，青砖石脚、坡形屋顶，1～2 楼层，内有小巧玲珑的庭园布局，大屋两侧各有一条青云巷。西关大屋体现了清代广州民居的特色。随着工商业发展和城区人口逐渐增多，19 世纪上半叶，广州开始出现竹筒屋，民国时期广州竹筒屋数量大增。竹筒屋开间小，进深大，呈纵长方形，宽为 4 米左右，进深少则七八米或十几米，多至 30 米以上，砖木结构，内设天井，生活空间相对独立。今日广州到处都是鳞次栉比的现代化住宅楼，传统的西关大屋和竹筒屋已为数不多了。

西关大屋内景。

The interior of the Xiguan Big House.

20世纪三四十年代广州竹筒屋门前。大门仍是广州民居中传统的双扇厚木门、趟栊门、脚门三件套。

The Bamboo tube houses of Guangzhou during 1930's and 1940's.The gate of such houses is typical Cantonese residential style which usually consists of 3 parts——the 2-leaf thick wooden doors, the sliding rail door and the foot door.

西关大屋内景。

The interior of the Xiguan big House.

雕刻精美的满洲窗。

The delicately engraved Manchuria window.

西关大屋客厅。

A Xiguan big House sitting room.

◎水上人家 Boat Dwellers

历史上珠江水上居民被称为“疍民”，或“疍家人”。他们长年泛舟江海，舟楫为家，以捕鱼拾蚝或渡客运货为生，漂泊无定。一家数口世代栖身在小舟中，即“连家船”，俗称“沙艇”。从前主要集结在长堤、黄沙一带的珠江水面，据统计，1926 年广州有水上居民 10.2 万人。新中国成立后，人民政府为水上居民建造了一批批陆上新居，现在绝大部分水上居民都在陆地定居，那种浮家泛宅的水上生活已成为过去。

20 世纪三四十年代广州珠江边的水上人家。

Pearl River fisherfolks in Guangzhou during 1930's and 1940's.

以船为家的孩子们。

Children in their boat houses.

◎花市 Flower Market

在广州人传统的岁时风俗中，除夕花市算得上是最具特色的场景。花市单作为买卖鲜花、花木的市场，起源于明万历年间。从清同治、光绪年间开始，逐渐发展为一年一度的迎春花市，成为广州特有的岁时风俗。从农历十二月廿八日至除夕中夜，连续3天的花市上除卖各色花卉外，还有很多工艺品展卖。逛花市是广州人除夕夜的重要活动内容，有“花海人潮十里长”之盛。

民国时期广州花市场景。《羊城竹枝词》曾这样描绘广州花市：“羊城世界本花花，更买鲜花度岁华。除夕案头齐供奉，香风吹暖到人家。”

A Guangzhou flower market in the period of the Republic of China.*On Bamboo and Flowers of Yangcheng* describes the Guangzhou flower market in this way, “In the colorful city of Guangzhou, people have the fine tradition of buying flowers in the New Year's eve and put them on the desks so that everyone smells the sweet fragrance of flowers everywhere.”

在粤语中，桃花的“桃”与鸿图的“图”谐音，插桃花象征来年鸿图大展，因此花市少不了桃花。当然，对年轻人来说，也有“行桃花运”之说。

In the Cantonese dialect, the word “tao” in “taohua” (“peach blossom”) has the same pronunciation as the word “tu” in “hongtu” (“good prospects”), therefore, there are usually lots of peach blossoms on sale before the New Year's Eve because arranging such flowers in a vase symbdizes boundless prospects, and especially for young people, being lucky in love affairs in the coming new year.

1938年除夕花市，在敌机空袭警报声中，广州市民依然踊跃购花。

In spite of the air raid alarm, Guangzhou citizens still go buying flowers in the flower market in the New Year's Eve of 1938.

◎舞狮 The Lion Dance

舞狮是模仿狮子形象动作的民间娱乐活动。广州舞狮属南狮，又称“醒狮”，明末就已在广东一带流行。广东醒狮头采用灯色扎作工艺，狮身覆以长丈余、宽4尺的图案狮被，以一人舞狮头，一人舞狮身，另一人戴大头佛面具，手摇葵扇，前导逗狮起舞。醒狮重“神似”，有文狮、武狮之分。文狮红脸白须，雄伟中见温文；武狮青面铁角牙刷须，豪放而粗犷。广州每逢节日或喜庆活动，都有舞狮表演，以示祥瑞。旧时舞狮队多由武馆组织。

20世纪30年代广州的舞狮场景。广州舞狮常有“狮子采青”，即用一竹竿吊起裹着利市的一扎生菜，“狮子”须有高超的技巧，上去将它咬取。

The Lion Dance in Guangzhou in 1930's. "Lion Picking up vegetable" is one of the Lion Dance programs in Guangzhou, during which the "lion" skillfully bites the bunch of vegetable (with Luck Money wrapped inside) tied to one end of a bamboo stick.

20世纪20年代广州街头的舞狮场面。

The Lion Dance in Guangzhou in 1920's.

20世纪30年代广州的舞狮场景。醒狮中文狮生动活泼，有搔痒舐毛、匍匐打滚等动作；武狮威武雄壮，有窜跃跌扑、上跃登高等动作。

The Lion Dance in Guangzhou in 1930's.The "Civil Lion" looks lively and energetic with different gestures of scratching, licking, crawling and rolling, while the "Military Lion" looks powerful and strong with various gestures of leaping, wrestling jumping and climbing.

◎舞龙 The Dragon Dance

舞龙又称舞龙灯，早在宋代就已十分流行，至今不衰。它是广州农村传统的喜庆游艺活动。舞龙结合了传统舞蹈和灯彩艺术，由一人手拿宝珠，在龙头前引龙起舞。龙头、龙身和龙尾一般用竹篾扎成，龙身从三节到几十节不等，多为单数，每节间以三至五尺绸布相连，再用色彩绘饰，节下装有木柄，供舞者握持，舞动时游龙如浪。节内燃烛者称“火龙”，鳞片贴金叶叫“金龙”，贴银片叫“银龙”，用禾草扎成的叫“草龙”。还有一种叫“烧龙”的，即在舞龙的同时，从龙口和龙身上喷出五彩缤纷的烟火，寓意烧掉秽气，迎来吉祥。

20世纪30年代广州越秀山体育场的舞龙场景。

The “Dragon Dance” in Yue xiushan Gym of Guangzhou in 1930's.

20世纪30年代广州街头的舞龙场面。

The "Dragon Dance" in Guangzhou street in 1930's.

◎划龙舟 Dragon Boat Racing

五月龙舟忙。划龙舟是广州端午节期间必不可少的民间传统活动，俗称“扒龙船”。通常是农历五月初一起龙船，初五举行赛龙舟。其时，珠江两岸观者聚集如云，所谓“龙船打龙鼓，咚咚响，响咚咚，江边看龙舟，口中吃住粽”。大的龙舟可坐 80 多人，桨手分左右两排而坐，由旗帜和锣鼓指挥，闻鼓则进，鸣锣则歇。

清末广州珠江上的划龙舟场面。船头装饰为龙头，有的耳目皆能活动，船尾装饰为龙尾。

The Dragon Boat Racing on the Pearl River of Guangzhou.The stem is usually decorated as a dragon head with moving dragon eyes and ears on both sides, while the stern as a dragon tail.

20世纪30年代龙舟赛一景。桥上、岸边万人涌动，观者如潮。

A Dragon Boat Racing in 1930's.There are thousands of visitors along the shore and on the bridge.

20世纪40年代珠江宽阔的江面上，龙腾虎跃的比赛场面。一艘龙舟，大的可长达30米，小的也有10多米长。

An intense and exciting dragon boat racing on the wide Pearl River in 1940's.A big dragon boat can be as long as 30 metres, while a smaller one can be 10 metres.

◎花轿 Sedan Chair

花轿是传统婚嫁仪式的象征，旧时女子总是以坐上大轿为身份改变、命运转折的真正开端。从前广州人办婚事可向专门经营仪仗事务的店铺预订花轿、高灯、大灯笼、彩亭、彩旗、八音锣鼓等一整套仪仗。花轿的行进有一套固定的程式：迎亲花轿和仪仗队伍按预定时辰抵达女家后，鼓乐齐鸣，新嫁娘便由大妗扶上花轿，再由父亲伯叔兄弟及亲族送行至半途，待男家喜席散后，新郎接轿等等。繁复的婚礼仪式在民国时期得到改革，很多人，尤其是知识阶层人士都实行所谓的“文明结婚”。1934 年 7 月，广州市政府发出《实施节约革除陋习规定》，其中对婚嫁仪式作了新的规定：迎亲时，“仪仗马色，一概废除”。花轿从此开始退出广州人的生活。

清末广州的花轿仪仗。

The bridal sedan chair and the honour guard in Guangzhou in the late Qing Dynasty.

民国时期的花轿。

The bridal sedan chair during the period of the Republic of China.

◎集体婚礼　Municipal Group Wedding Ceremony

婚嫁仪式是社会风尚的一种体现，民国时期，广州市政府已开始提倡改良传统的婚嫁仪式。1935 年 12 月 1 日，广州市举办了有 79 对新婚夫妇参加的首届集体婚礼，当时称“集团婚礼”，广州市社会局局长张远峰代替市长刘纪文充任证婚人。婚礼仪式包括了由证婚人率新婚夫妇向国旗和孙中山遗像行三鞠躬礼以及新婚夫妇相互行三鞠躬礼、由证婚人向新人颁发结婚证书、由证婚人致词以及礼毕后合影等。民国时期，广州市共举办了 9 届集体婚礼。

1935 年广州市第一届集团婚礼。婚礼结束后，新人们与家属在广州市政府合署大楼前合影。

The 1st Guangzhou Mass Wedding in 1935.The new couples and their families have a group photo taken in front of the Government Comprehensive Building of Guangzhou City after the ceremony.

新婚夫妇在司仪的带领下开始出场。

The young couple led by the ceremony master.

广州市第一届集团婚礼上的一对新人。

A young couple in the 1st Guangzhou Mass Wedding.

◎丧礼 Funerals

“亡灵一去永无踪，生死阴阳路不同。若要相逢难见面，除非梦里笑谈中。”尽管人死如灯灭，但从前的丧礼却极其繁复，有报丧、入殓、设灵、吊孝、出殡、安葬以及祭祀等一整套程序。

灵堂，俗称“孝堂”，设死者的遗像和神主牌，供香炉、烛台、长明灯、供品，悬挂挽联、哀帏等。图为民国时期广州人家丧事灵堂的布置。

Mourning hall arrangement of Guangzhou common people during the period of the Republic of China.The mourning hall, also called the worship hall, has a photo of the deceased and the tablet of spirit, as well as the incense burner, the candlesticks, the everlighting lamps, the offerings, the elegiac couplets, and the elegiac curtains.

出殡是当事人家的门面，极其隆重，有一整套仪仗：金鼓、大蓝灯笼、生花牌、生花圈、纸扎装饰品、香烛酒肴亭、管弦乐手、唢呐、锣鼓，还请有打梵乐的僧尼等，抬柩人数视棺柩大小而定，4至8人以至更多不等。图为民国时期广州出殡仪仗的场面。

Funeral is a ceremony.There were a set of properties: golden drums, big blue lanterns, flower boards, wreaths, paper decorations, pavilion filled with candles, wine and food, orchestra and so on.The family of the deceased also requested monks or nuns to play Buddist music.The number of the people carrying coffin ranged from 4 to 8.The photo shows the funeral scenes in Guangzhou during the Republic of China.

“死人灯笼报大数”，举着蓝灯笼和花圈的队伍，故意夸大逝者寿数。

“The number of lanterns for the deceased inflate their age.” As the saying goes, the procession that carries blue lanterns and wreathes always exagerates the actual age of the deceased.

◎禁娼 Banning Prostitutes

从前广州娼妓有妓寨、妓艇、妓庵三类。清末民初，广州娼妓最盛，公私娼妓遍及全市。公娼向税务、警察部门缴纳“花捐”，以合法身份公开营业。私娼则多凭借地方势力、黑社会组织或与不法军警相勾结而获得生存。社会有识之士多次呼吁废娼，并举行过请愿游行，但娼妓始终不绝。据 1948 年不完全统计，广州当时以卖淫为生的妇女有 8000～9000 人。

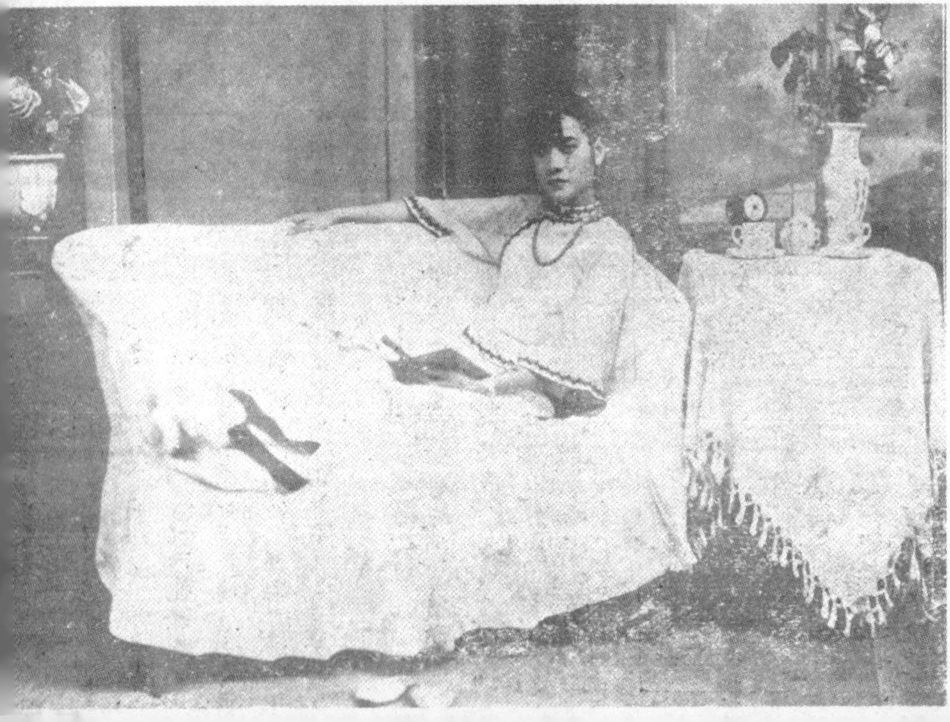

20 世纪 30 年代的广州妓女。

A Prostitute in Guangzhou in 1930's.

广州沦陷时期公开的妓馆。

The open brothel in Guangzhou during the period of time when Guangzhou was occupied by the Japanese troops.

1922 年 4 月 1 日，广州各界废娼请愿大游行的队伍。

On Apr.1st, 1922, people of all fields in Guangzhou had a demonstration against prostitution.

◎禁赌　Gambling Banning

清末广州有公开的“围姓”和“番摊”赌博。“围姓”是以赴考者姓氏作猜赌对象，除去大姓，限猜其他小姓，以揭榜为据，这种赌博随科举制度废除而消失。民国时期广州还有“山票”、“铺票”、“白鸽票”、“字花”、“牌九”、“鱼虾蟹”、“骰宝”等赌博形式。清末，广州曾一度禁赌。民国期间广州各界多次呼吁禁赌，政府当局则屡禁屡放。据不完全统计，1949 年 5 月，广州市共有赌档 2000 多，以赌为生者 3 万余人。

“番摊”是赌博的一种形式。将铜钱或小瓷片或扁豆作为“摊皮”，从中拨出一小堆放到摊盅里，猜赌为博，流行于下层。图为民国初年广州“番摊”聚赌场面。

The “Fantan Gambling” in Guangzhou in the early period of the Republic of china. “Fantan” is a kind of popular gambling among lower class people.Gamblers always put copper coins or small porcelain pieces, or hyaccinth beans in a pot to start their gambling.

1920年11月23日，广州禁赌请愿大巡行的场面。

A demonstration against gambling in Guangzhou in Nov.23, 1920.

1936年9月，广州实行禁赌后被封的一家赌场。

In September 1936, a casino was closed because of gambling banning in Guangzhou.

广州沦陷时期街头公开赌博的人们。

People still gambled in the street when Guangzhou was occupied by the Japanese troops.

◎禁毒 Drug Banning

鸦片战争期间，林则徐在虎门当众销毁鸦片 230 多万斤。但鸦片战争后，鸦片仍源源不断流入广州。民国期间，政府当局也曾查禁鸦片，但很多时候却是明禁暗纵，禁烟机构常常卖烟。广州刚解放时，市区还有烟馆 1300 多档。

清末广州的鸦片烟馆。“睡横床、吹直竹，不管老婆子女哭；倾家荡产，卖田卖屋”是当时的社会写照。广州人称烟枪为“大辘藕”，故抽大烟称为“食大辘藕”。

The opium house in Guangzhou in the late Qing Dynasty.The opium smokers, “lying in bed smoking opium all day, leaving aside the crying of wives and kids, are reduced to poverty and ruin after selling all fields and houses”, which reflects the social situation of that time.Smoking opium is colloquially called “eating big lotus” because the opium pipe is also called “ big lotus” by the Guangzhou people.

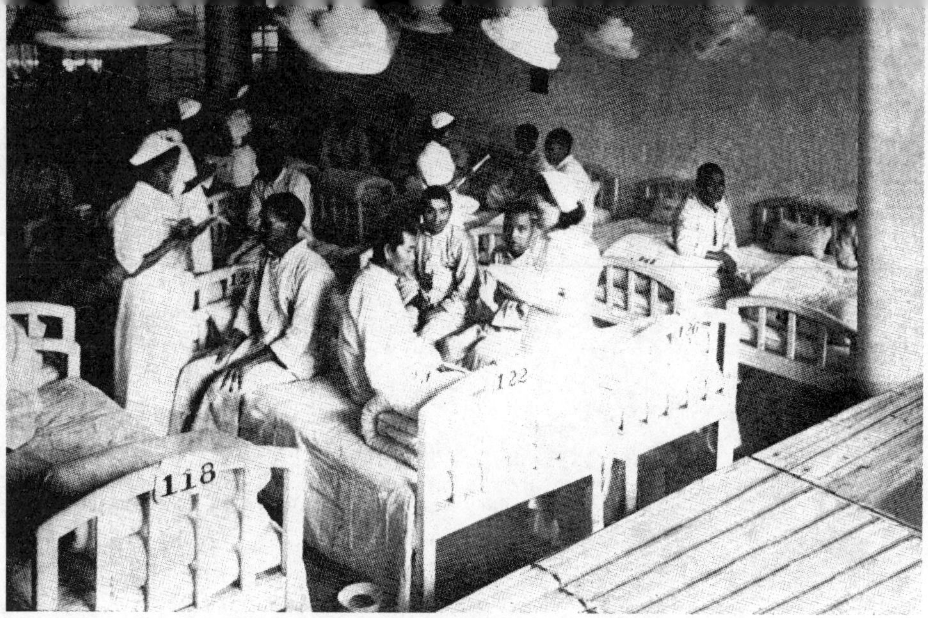

20世纪30年代广州市戒烟医院的病房。

The ward of a giving-up-opium hospital in Guangzhou in 1930's.

1937年广州市宣传禁毒活动的化装游行。

A fancy dress parade to propagate drug banning in Guangzhou in 1937.

烟枪、烟灯、匿烟物等都是吸鸦片的必要工具。烟枪以旧物为贵，多为竹制，枪头裹以金银锡，枪口亦饰以珠宝、玉器、金箔。烟灯上有铜盖，罩以玻璃，中储以油，燃棉纱为芯，明灯后即可以烟枪就火吸食。图为 1941 年广东禁烟局焚毁私烟器具场面。

The Guangdong Opium Ban Department had the smoking paraphernalias burnt in 1941.The opium pipe, opium lamp and pipe bowl are all necessary smoking sets.The opium pipe, mainly made of bamboo, is more expensive if it's an old one.The pipe head is wrapped in gold, silver and tin, while the pipe muzzle is decorated with jewels, jade and goldleaf.The opium lamp, which has a copper lid, is covered by glass.Opium oil is put inside together with a cotton core.Opium is smoked through the pipe after the lamp is lit.

后记

《老广州》原名《羊城寻旧》，内容包括街市景观、名胜古迹、经济掠影、教育概况、社会生活和民生习俗六个部分，以图文对照方式，介绍旧时广州的社会文化风貌。本书自 2004 年出版以来，一直是各大书店常销书。

为促进广州对外文化交流，满足读者需求，我们将原《羊城寻旧》图文内容进行修订和补充，增加图片英文说明，邀请著名文化人刘斯奋赠序并题写书名，易书名为《老广州》。愿本书能使海内外朋友在轻松阅读中获益，祈望广大读者继续对本书提出宝贵意见。

编著者